THE LIBRARY
The Library is operated by UU Bibliotech Ltd, a wholly owned subsidiary company of the University of Ulster

University of Ulster at Magee

Due Back (subject to recall)

1 8 MAR 2007		

Fines will apply to items returned after due date

GERTRUD BODENWIESER AND VIENNA'S CONTRIBUTION TO AUSDRUCKSTANZ

Choreography and Dance Studies

A series of books edited by Muriel Topaz and Robert P. Cohan, CBE

Please see the back of this book for other titles in the Choreography and Dance Studies series

GERTRUD BODENWIESER AND VIENNA'S CONTRIBUTION TO AUSDRUCKSTANZ

Edited by
Bettina Vernon-Warren
and
Charles Warren

harwood academic publishers
Australia • Canada • China • France • Germany
India • Japan • Luxembourg • Malaysia • The Netherlands
Russia • Singapore • Switzerland

Amsteldijk 166
1st Floor
1079 LH Amsterdam
The Netherlands

British Library Cataloguing in Publication Data

Gertrud Bodenwieser and Vienna's contribution to
    Ausdruckstanz. – (Choreography and dance studies; v. 18)
    1. Bodenwieser, Gertrud   2. Choreography – Austria – Vienna –
    History
    I. Vernon-Warren, Bettina   II. Warren, Charles
    792.8'2'092

    ISBN 90-5755-035-0

Cover illustration: Gertrud Bodenwieser and Illa Raudnitz in *Gekreuzte Linien (Crossed Lines)*, 1928. Watercolor sketch by Felix Albrecht Harta.

CONTENTS

INTRODUCTION TO THE SERIES

Choreography and Dance Studies is a book series of special interest to dancers, dance teachers and choreographers. Focusing on dance composition, its techniques and training, the series will also cover the relationship of choreography to other components of dance performance such as music, lighting and the training of dancers.

In addition, *Choreography and Dance Studies* will seek to publish new works and provide translations of works not previously published in English, as well as to publish reprints of currently unavailable books of outstanding value to the dance community.

Muriel Topaz
Robert P. Cohan

APPRECIATIONS

Evelyn Ippen's long partnership with Bettina Vernon as a dancer and choreographer has been of inestimable value and has played an equal part in their joint ventures. The immense contribution made by June Layson as prime instigator of this book is gratefully acknowledged; likewise the assistance of Christian Lanzer, particularly in respect of the translations, and the contributions of Marcel Lorber and Leslie Moorhouse, principal advisers, composers and pianists for many years.

The encouragement and help received from the following organisations and individuals throughout Evelyn's and Bettina's joint careers have been greatly appreciated, thereby facilitating the publication of this book: Andrea Amort; Anglo-Austrian Society; Arts Council of Great Britain (previously CEMA, now Arts Council of England); Australian Council for the Arts (now Australia Council); Australian High Commission; Austrian Cultural Institute; Austrian Embassy; Austrian Theater Museum; Gerhard Brunner; Bunzl plc; Clement Crisp; Concert Artist Promotions Ltd; Concert Management Pty. Ltd; *The Dancing Times*; Nicholas Dromgoole; Arthur Fleischmann; Walter Foster; Esther Linley; Ministry of Education, Australia; Alfred Oberzaucher and Gunhild Oberzaucher-Schüller; Sadler's Wells Theatre; Society for Dance Research; *Tanz Affiche*; Theatre Museum, London; University of Surrey; Jarmila Weissenböck; and Grete Wiesenthal.

Finally, special thanks to Patricia Grayburn, Arts Administrator, University of Surrey, not only for her contributions, but also for her valuable assistance with translation, for editing the manuscript and for preparing the index.

LIST OF PLATES

FOREWORD

In memoriam Bettina Vernon-Warren
by Clement Crisp

I owe my understanding of Gertrud Bodenwieser to Bettina Vernon, and naturally enough, my knowledge and admiration of Bettina Vernon's dancing to Gertrud Bodenwieser. In 1947/8 I saw Bettina Vernon and Evelyn Ippen in their *Ballet for Two* performances. "Ballet" seemed something of a misnomer, for their dance style was nearer Jooss than Ashton to my eyes; however, their dancing had all the virtues one might admire in the best dancers (at Sadler's Wells and Rambert) of that time. Bettina Vernon, to whom I also owe my presence as writer of this foreword, moved with a wonderful simplicity and a full-toned power. She was intensely feminine, lovely, and her Wiesenthal/Bodenwieser heritage suited and focused her gifts. These meant a lilt and a rhythmic subtlety – I might say a rhythmic charm – to her movement, which told of an unerring feeling for the music and a delicate response to it. (You can see it, sense it, albeit at second hand, in reconstructions of *Mermaid* and *Voices of Spring*.) Her dancing seemed radiant and apparently spontaneous though, as I came to know Bettina Vernon in latter years, I recognised that she was far too much of a professional and a theater creature to believe in spontaneity in performance. Nearly fifty years later, as we lunched one day and discussed a lecture demonstration that she was to give, Bettina Vernon started to show me part of one of her dances. The delicious curve of *épaulement*, a sense, a hint, of movement being born and then starting to flower, was immensely touching as it brought back memories of her stage appearances.

About Gertrud Bodenwieser she spoke, of course, with immense feeling and understanding. My own early impressions of Bodenwieser as a creator and, very importantly, as an educational visionary (witness her fascinating letter to *The Dancing Times* in 1929) were also confirmed in talking to Arnold Haskell. Haskell had, from the 1920s, recognised Bodenwieser's significance and was later to be a great admirer of Bettina Vernon and Evelyn Ippen.

Most of Bodenwieser's dances are now ghosts, faintly glimpsed in photographs and critical comment. Thanks to the devotion of Bettina Vernon and Evelyn Ippen, some are more than specters. To savor them, to understand them, we need to look at what Bettina Vernon sought in dancing when she taught them, and what she gave to dancing: movement strong in pulse, subtle in rhythm, full-bodied in its involvement with its text. Dancing today, in classical ballet or in modern and post-modern style, is increasingly fast, aerodynamically efficient, hard-driven, extreme in shape. It can also, in the creations of such dubious luminaries as William Forsythe, Stephen Petronio and their ilk, look brutish. The Bodenwieser style, the Vernon style, offered something much more inward, with a sense of emotional and physical weight that is sadly neglected in ballet performance as in modern and post-modern stagings, notably when interpreting the work of earlier generations. The heirs betray their ancestors: Petipa is high-kicked out of shape; Martha Graham is made slick.

In performance and reconstruction, Gertrud Bodenwieser's work, and Bettina Vernon's invaluable rescue of it, must be accorded a sensitive feeling for the shape and weight of the dances and their musical impulse. We owe it to Bettina Vernon's memory to insist upon these fine dance qualities: they were hers as an artist, and we will sense her gifts once again if we respect what she brought to Bodenwieser and then showed so splendidly to a new generation.

IN TRIBUTE

The impetus for this book arose from discussions between Bettina Vernon and myself. Bettina Vernon, the former Bodenwieser dancer and, until her death on 5 June 1995, a leading protagonist and exponent of the Bodenwieser modern dance style, wanted to ensure that Bodenwieser's work and place in the development of *Ausdruckstanz* would be widely known and appreciated. While I was Head of the Department of Dance Studies at the University of Surrey, I invited Bettina Vernon to visit the university on a regular basis to work with postgraduate students in the reconstruction of some of Bodenwieser's dances and to initiate further study of her work.

Bettina Vernon, 1991

A logical outcome of these profitable interactions was to embark upon a book which would also both inform and promote Bodenwieser's work. Sadly, Bettina Vernon did not live to see this book in its published form; however, she had full editorial responsibility up to the time of her death. This volume, therefore, is a tribute to Bettina Vernon and her constant enthusiasm and commitment to dance.

June Layson

1 *Cakewalk*, choreographed and danced by Bodenwieser in 1919. One of Bodenwieser's first choreographies.

INTRODUCTION

Gertrud Bodenwieser (born Vienna, 1890; died Sydney, 1959) was a modern dance choreographer, performer and teacher. As such she is usually mentioned in dance histories, dictionaries and encyclopedias although rarely is attention paid in detail to either her work or place within the development of *Ausdruckstanz*, the modern dance style with which she is associated.

This text focuses on Gertrud Bodenwieser and does so in several different ways. It is neither a biography nor a systematic account of her oeuvre, performance style or dance technique. This is not to deny that these areas are in need of exploration; indeed one of the outcomes of such a publication is the many lines of further investigation and research which suggest themselves. Rather, in this collection of writings each contributor highlights Bodenwieser's achievements from a different perspective. Such a unique approach allows the reminiscences of Bodenwieser's pupils and company members (later choreographers, performers and teachers in their own right) to take their place immediately alongside the essays of the dance scholars and academics.

The result is a text which covers Bodenwieser's life from early Viennese influences to her private solo début in 1919 (when she was twenty-nine years of age), her subsequent nearly two decades of great creativity and then her emigration to Australia after the *Anschluss* (the annexation of Austria by Nazi Germany in 1938). While the time span provides a loose framework it is crisscrossed and illuminated by the various interests pursued by the authors, including detailed accounts of some of Bodenwieser's choreographic works, memories of being taught by her, and dancing in her companies.

All this, though, may beg the question of why a dance artist such as Bodenwieser, eminent in her time and, working in the two widely separated continents, should have slipped into relative international dance obscurity less than fifty years after her death.

The first answer to this question is true of much of dance and its protagonists. Dance is the most ephemeral of the performing arts, mainly because of the lack hitherto of a universally accepted notation system. It is only now that it is benefitting from the increasingly widespread use of notation as a recording tool, as well as the innovative approaches that video and computers promote. Bodenwieser's work largely pre-dates these developments and it lives on only in the experience of her surviving dancers, the few reconstructions that have been made of key works, and the writings of German and Austrian scholars. The latter are largely unavailable in English translation.

More importantly, the second reason for the absence of an extant amount of Bodenwieser's choreography and a subsequent critical body of writings is the result of the Holocaust. Destructive of cultures, artefacts and records, as well as entire groups of people, it caused much documentary evidence relating to Bodenwieser to be lost. Furthermore, unlike other dance theorists, choreographers and performers of the immediate pre-Second World War diaspora such as Rudolf von Laban (to the U.K.) or George Balanchine (to the U.S.A), Bodenwieser did not emigrate to a culturally dance-akin country or continent. While Bodenwieser's contemporaries picked up the threads of their pre-emigration careers quickly, if not always entirely seamlessly or in exactly the same direction, Bodenwieser virtually started afresh when she settled in Australia. Although she had the nucleus of her company with her, together with a substantial oeuvre, the new context was one in which modern dance was almost unknown and devoid of indigenous roots. She was both artistically and literally far-removed from the nourishing climate of Vienna and the burgeoning European modern dance scene. Even so, much of the little that has been written about Bodenwieser stems from this final period of self-exile.

Any attempt to examine and assess the work of a dance personality without recourse to full archival evidence is fraught with problems. The text endeavors to meet some of these difficulties. It gives equal prominence to the testimonies of those who knew Bodenwieser, worked with her and matured as performers and teachers under her guidance and to those who, subsequently, have studied and analyzed what little documentary evidence remains. This places particular responsibilities on the reader since such disparate writing cannot be engaged with in the same manner throughout. It requires awareness of and sensitivity to the different kinds of comment, description and opinion presented.

It may, therefore, be helpful to the reader to appreciate that the elements of this text can be grouped into four categories, even if this is not immediately apparent in the structure.

Firstly, the chronology and the choreochronicle provide the essential time and place parameters to Bodenwieser's life and work. Such 'fixings' of events are necessary since they offer a scaffolding within which study can proceed. Even so, some dates and locations are uncorroborated, many more are unknown and the need persists for such documentation to be continued. In particular, the whole range of details of Bodenwieser's many performances throughout Europe and wider afield is lacking. Without this information even basic documentary work, such as the frequency of performances of a particular dance (an indication of its popularity, ease of touring, etc.) and duration in the repertoire (essential if a study of choreographic style is to be pursued), is thwarted.

Secondly, the witting testimonies of Bodenwieser's former pupils and members of her companies stand apart from the chronology and the choreochronicle. Although the dates mentioned and the events described can be cross-referenced with the charts, the value of such statements lies in the very experiences remembered and related. Of course, human memory is neither infallible nor unselective and must be accepted as such, but the eye-witness accounts, the 'I was there', the 'I lived through and experienced this' modes are invaluable. Another characteristic of these personal accounts is that inevitably they overlap in their descriptions. In this text such apparent repetitions have merit since they present the reader with an unusual opportunity to approach Bodenwieser's work through varying viewpoints and, possibly, to gain a deeper understanding than might otherwise be the case. The point being maintained here is that such personal and subjective perspectives are all equally valid and, collectively, highly prized as points of departure for further study and thought. This is primary source material of the first order.

Thirdly, the contributions of the professional dance writers, properly considered as secondary source material, provide insights not gained elsewhere in the text. Here scholars who have worked in this area of study for many years bring their knowledge and understanding of Bodenwieser's work to the point that, from a basis of documentation and description, analyses are made, interpretations offered and evaluations proposed.

Fourthly, at key points throughout the text unique visual archival material is presented. The reproductions of programmes, press photographs and other performance details, together with documentary evidence relating to Bodenwieser's School, provide arresting insights to her work. Here the artistic veracity of her choreography, its rootedness in *Ausdruckstanz* and the prevailing aesthetic, social and political concerns are manifest. This wealth of visual material offers invaluable complementary statements to the text.

Nevertheless the text is presented in a non-didactic manner. Its concerns are to make Bodenwieser's work and contribution to *Ausdruckstanz* in particular, and modern dance and dance theater in general, available for further scrutiny and comment.

The fact that relatively little is known about Bodenwieser points to the opportunities for sustained research efforts. Detailed studies of Bodenwieser's choreographic style, her abilities as a performer and her development and teaching of her specific dance technique are immediate potential areas for study. Within a wider focus, Bodenwieser's links with drama and multi-media stage productions and the degree to which she was influenced by the unique Viennese artistic and cultural milieux are other avenues to be explored. It would be illuminating, too, to pursue specific theoretical approaches, such as that provided by a feminist-inspired history methodology.

In the 1920s and 1930s Gertrud Bodenwieser was considered to be a leading exponent of *Ausdruckstanz*, with a definitive personal style and a philosophy of dance that distinguished her from her contemporaries. It is for the reader to discover some of the reasons why this was so in the following text.

June Layson

PART I

BODENWIESER'S INSPIRATIONS

1

VIENNA: TO GIVE AN INKLING OF ITS NATURE AND CULTURE

George Jackson

To set the tone, here is a fragment from a story, a tale, not out of the Vienna Woods but the Prater, an amusement park and nature reserve within Vienna's city limits.

"The first Black the boy had seen surprised him. The hair of the man's head and beard was absolutely white. His clothes were formal for an outing into the open air. Sitting on a bench at the edge of a grassy expanse, reading a book, the white-haired black-skinned man's posture was so upright, so imposing that he looked like an emperor. 'An African emperor!' the boy exclaimed to the family cook who, exceptionally, was his guardian for this afternoon walk. 'No, he's a professor and from America, I've seen him before'. The cook's reply was uttered in a guilty whisper, but she wasn't really ashamed of having nosed about in something that was none of her business because she had never seen a black person, nor a yellow, until she'd left her Moravian town to work for Jews in Vienna."[1]

Different races aware of each other, different social classes in discreet contact are part and parcel of legendary Vienna. So are other examples of diversity and of opposites in delicate balance: "but the boy had grander things on his mind than professors, of whom he knew a number in his family and among his parents' friends... Leaving the Prater's meadows and chestnut alleys, the pair emerged from under a railway viaduct to face Admiral Tegethoff's column and dodge trams at the Praterstern, hub of several radial avenues. They crossed to a broad street named after the author of the boy's favourite poem, *The Lorelei*. This thoroughfare funnelled them between long house blocks to a narrow cross street named for the circus. It led, indeed, to a building, part ostentation and part secrets, in front of whose portals, whenever the circus was in town, men in uniforms of vivid colour, with epaulets and much gold braid, made themselves important. These figures were arch-dukes and princes in the boy's imagination, although he'd found out long ago at a performance that they were only doormen and ushers. Yet, the illusion persisted...". Life in Vienna took place amidst calculated

2   The Vienna Secession[2] Exhibition Building. The famous art nouveau building erected by Joseph Olbrich for the group of avant-garde artists founded in 1897.

juxtapositions of nature and architecture, among memorials to the past ringed by novel items of engineering, within the clash of imperial royal fantasies with fact hushed as gossip, and in a context of showmanship displayed even at the street kerb.

In deciding on a chapter about Vienna for a publication which explores the life and work of the Viennese/Sydneyite modern dancer Gertrud Bodenwieser, an assumption was made: that an artist's native city is an important factor in creativity. If, however, one considers such modern phenomena as the alienation of the urban persona and the influence of mass communications from outside the community, doubts begin to arise concerning a necessary connection between not only an individual's productivity but any distinctive aspect of personal character and the civic environment. Of course, one may try to discover or dispute such connections, but this can be done only on a case by case basis. In Bodenwieser's case, the task is saved for later chapters. Meanwhile, let's treat the assumption of Vienna's significance for its inhabitants as an act of faith.

Vienna from 1890 to 1938

The city into which Gertrud Bodenwieser was born in 1890 differed in important but not all respects from the one she left definitively in 1938. In 1890, it was a large (more than 2 million population), diverse (multinational, although Germanoaustrians were in the majority; multiclass, with older as well as newer social orders), traditionalist (conservative but, by subsequent standards, tolerant) imperial capital. Yet in feeling, Vienna seemed circumscribed. To think of it as small townish would be an exaggeration. Rather, it was a comfortable, contained city, not a massive one. The architectural grandeur of the Gründerzeit (the 1860s era of the founders of capitalist, industrialist, commercial undertakings within an imperial landed society) was limited. It was restricted by a building code and circular city plan, as well as by the open ring of hills and low mountains that, at some remove, edged in the citizens' view in several directions. What impinged on one's senses and sensibility in Vienna was due to both human design and natural topography.

Even today, to stand on a "typical" Viennese thoroughfare is to become aware of features that haven't changed in over a hundred years. The shape of the houses, be they recent or venerable, and of the entire street has remained constant. The houses merge into a block form, longer than high. This oblong has a certain mass, but avoids being heavy because prominent features of the house façades are windows. They occur as individual units in repetitive rows. Frequently the window-frames are neoclassical, composed of columns or indications thereof, with capitals, cornices, even triangular pediments, each resembling a miniature of an ancient temple. Yet together, in straight lines, these window rows seem to parade like Lipizzaner stallions making an entrée on to the coffee colored turf of the Imperial Castle's Spanish Riding School, or like the defile of the corps in the ballet *Fairy Doll* on to the stage of the Court, later State, Opera House. Looking down the street, there is a uniformity of building height, a seamless, rulered perspective. Above the street is the sky, very apparent because it is severed so cleanly from human habitation by the evenness of the rooftops, and in the distance, perhaps, appears a vineyard's slope or a wooded hilltop.

Seeing these housefronts, walking such streets, and living in this setting, one may well become susceptible to their proportions and mood. The proportions inculcate not just a particular sense of extremes (what is near and what is far, or big or small, what is dense or what seems an expanse), but also what constitutes the proper balance. The mood, distilled from the wistful play of light on outside walls plastered in tints of foal grey, foam white or carmelized yellow and from the etiquette imposed by great entrance doors leading to steep stairhalls, is utterly urban and rather civilized.

In 1890, in 1938, and today, Vienna was and remains a more traditionalist city than any number of its peers. It happens in this city that nextdoor neighbours lead lives which, at some levels, belong to different centuries. Of course, there are links: "Into old glass/new wine is filled."[3] Innovation, which between 1890 and 1938 thrived in the arts, sciences, scholarship, and commerce, and incubated in politics, grew out of precedents and solid traditions rather than from alternative sources. Although the various Viennese establishments had their opponents, there was no proper counterculture. There were "Vienna schools" of music, ethnology, design and philosophy, indicating that the critical mass for creativity was more than ample. Because art and science were linked, no "two cultures" enmity existed between their practitioners. Revolutionary artists received their training in academic styles and techniques, scientists attended plays and formed amateur music groups with lawyers and doctors. The difference between high art and popular fare was acknowledged, but not strictly observed. The poorer classes, too, attended theaters, took part in parades, and indulged in the masquerades that remained important in the city's official and social life.

It was not literally true that one could meet everyone of importance in any field of endeavor, yet the members of one's circle probably had done so *in toto*. As late as the 1930s, this or that relation or family friend played chamber music with the good amateur Einstein, had studied singing with opera star Maria Jeritza's less famous but "even more musical" sister, took courses from Freud, appeared in a film with beauty Hedy Kiesler soon to be Lamarr, was novelist Felix Salten's physician, socialized with conductor Bruno Walter's daughters, had gone to social dance class with future film star Francis Lederer, had attended primary school with ballerina-to-be Gusti Pichler, was a medical colleague of doctor-composer Ernst Toch, and so on. For a Viennese, such a list wasn't namedropping but part of an everyday litany that maintained one's "connections".

As a population center, Vienna declined slightly from its imperial to republican days. There were somewhat fewer than 2 million people in the 1930s. Nor in those years did the city alter much in area; however, the feeling of the place changed. Until quite late into modern times, the imperial House of Hapsburg had kept Vienna purposely small and walled to limit the land holdings of other noble families in what it considered to be its city. After the walls came down in the 1860s, the Gründerzeit building boom was one of both quantity and concept, but, as already noted, it was a boom contained within limits. As the capital of a farflung empire, the Vienna of the second portion of the long reign of Franz Josef (Emperor of Austria, King of Hungary – hence "Imperial Royal") was a modest metropolis, whereas after 1918, as the capital of a tiny republic, Vienna was "too big". Yet, for more than a decade, until the first republic's second economic crisis in 1930–1, it came to seem more and more cosmopolitan. Nevertheless, it hadn't (except during carnival) a big nightlife like Paris or Berlin, nor a population of devoted club-members at all levels (such as London's leisured gentlemen's clubs, garden clubs, laborers' cooperatives). Instead, Vienna had the afternoon coffeehouse habit, or in fine weather took supper at suburban winegardens.

During imperial times, court functions determined the policies and etiquette that filtered down through government bureaux and elegant salons to burgherly businesses and house parties and to work sites and folk fests. Knowledge and taste, though, could also percolate up. Princess Pauline Metternich's liberal salon set artistic and even scientific policy at the turn of the century. In republican days, when salons became unaffordable, one met people almost exclusively on mutual ground: out, not at home. That so much of social life was conducted in public gave the Viennese a theatrical sensibility. The feeling of always giving a performance was abetted by adherence to old-fashioned social, civic and religious ceremonies and though these could be somewhat dour, they were buffered by the longing for *Gemütlichkeit* (which began as a neither unwitty nor undignified sense of ease, but was corrupted into "being comfy"). In Vienna, formal manners and relaxed habits were in harmony, not in counterpoint.

Besides coffeehouses, favorite meeting places in Vienna included the ice-skating rink and the bath house. A tale from the Vienna baths reminds us that these institutions weren't just for cleanliness and health. "Everything about the Baths of Diana, its columned halls and tiled pools, was classical and pagan, save its lift. The contraption that raised one from the parterre to those Olympian heights of bayleaf-scented steam clouds and lapping waters was a device of torture veritably medieval in spirit. People were so afraid of riding it that they remembered their immortal souls and uttered a prayer. With most of Vienna being Catholic, the usual prayer was the Pater Noster, thus the device became known as a pater noster. Passenger boxes, dark as coffins, upright and one atop another, moved through a pair of shafts up the first, down the second. They never stopped. You had to jump in and out. To hesitate a moment before entering merely meant that you waited for the following coffin, but to hesitate before exiting meant that you had missed your floor ... They felt a pause, a tremor and then the cabin moved sideways. Again the sound changed. They were beginning to descend without having been turned upside down, yet the boy continued to cling to her and didn't let go. He held her as he hadn't held his mother since he was little. She unfastened his grasp, yet keeping hold of one of his hands pulled him forward, commanding him to jump. 'We'd have missed our floor again if I'd let you stand there any longer', she said laughing. 'You're still shaking. Come, change your clothes in my room. You're much too excited to be left alone.'" Flirtation and seduction were interwoven in Vienna with gossip and intellectual debate. All were practised in public places.

It is remarkable that between 1848 and 1938 so many people who became famous, or infamous, around the world, lived in Vienna. The city was particularly pre-eminent in music and medicine, yet it was also rich in literature and physics, the plastic arts and philosophy, economics, architecture, theater and puppetry, banking and aspects of industry. Of those who achieved a "name", some were born in Vienna, others were attracted to it as if by honey and spent their lives there or returned repeatedly. Some, after the *Anschluss*, paid with their lives because they couldn't tear themselves away.

It wasn't just talents of the first order that were a distinctive lot. In Vienna, style permeated the ranks and fostered individuality (often without eccentricity) among the least famous in each field. Perhaps in those years this was because of the city's balance of culture and nature, its basis for innovation in tradition, the conduct of so much private life in public, and a consensus on what remained implied and what was made explicit. There may have been an exception, though, for people who were to cause political things to happen (Masaryk, Fried, Herzl, Hitler, Trotsky,

Stalin and the visiting Lenin). For them, Vienna was more of a waiting place. (The exception to this exception was Karl Lueger, Vienna's populist mayor from 1897–1910 whom some consider a prototype Hitler. Lueger's field of action, however, did not extend much beyond the city.)

The names of famous Viennese are legion. Between the 1860s and 1930s three seminal composers lived in Vienna – Brahms, Johann Strauss and Schönberg – and two visited – Wagner and Offenbach. Their followers included other stars. Which among them was the most Viennese, a resident like Bruckner, Mahler or Wolf, or the transient Richard Strauss? And why didn't the music of Franz Schmidt, Josef Matthias Hauer or Alexander von Zemlinsky become as famous in the world as in Vienna, whereas that of Webern, Berg and Krenek did? For visual artists, Vienna was less of a magnet than Paris, but those who worked in Vienna before World War II have since, gradually, gained international renown: the opulently academic Makart of the Gründerzeit; the Hapsburgs' sensitive realist Rudolf von Alt who invented expressionism to distract himself from a toothache; the sensual pre-Cubist Klimt; and true modernists like electric Schiele, magnetic Kokoschka, radioactive Gerstl. Many a Viennese author (the 19th century's Grillparzer, Hebbel and Stifter, and into or in the 20th, Musil, Trakl, Werfel, Stefan Zweig, Wildgans, Kraus, Altenberg, Broch, Roth, Horvath) was translated in the 1950s and '60s. Many are still periodically reread elsewhere than in Vienna; Hofmannsthal seems to endure because of his opera libretti for Richard Strauss, and Schnitzler because of his Freudian appeal. Science is supposed to be more objective and universal than art, yet there are those who find Viennese aspects not just in the lives, but also in the work of the great practitioners of medicine, psychiatry and psychology (Semmelweis, Billroth, Krafft-Ebing, Freud, Weininger, Frisch, Lorenz); even also in the outstanding physicists (Boltzmann, Mach, Schrödinger, Meitner), because of their disposition to philosophize and psychologize the facts. These scientists tended to be both specialists and generalists. No one disputes that philosophers (Brentano, Wittgenstein, Husserl, or Carnap and his colleagues in the Vienna Circle), economists (Hayek) and architects (Loos, Otto Wagner, Hoffmann, Neutra, Kiesler) or designers (the members of the Wiener Werkstätte[4]) have style; critics (the always old Hanslick, Edwin Denby who was to remain ever young, Walter Sorell who grew more youthful each year) and theater and film directors (Reinhardt, Ophuls, Pabst, Preminger, Lang, Wilder, Viertel, Stroheim) certainly do. These are only some of the many whose encounter with Vienna was significant.

Many have speculated why Vienna changed, why its sense of balance was upset. Was it removal of the emperor at one end of the scale or, at the other, replacement of an educated underclass by a know-nothing rural mentality that led to Germanification? (Some think Vienna at the turn of the century had history's best educated poor.) If there had not been a push from outside by Hitler, the Austrian, from his German seat of power, would Vienna in its old-fashioned way have retained its diversified and cosmopolitan character? Or would it, of itself, led by successors to Lueger and Dollfuss, have become more Germanic, totalitarian and provincially up-to-date?

What happened wasn't gradual. Overnight, with the *Anschluss*, Vienna ceased to be a capital. It became less diverse, less free. The social fabric, which previously had held despite outbursts of nationalist and class violence, was torn. "'You look like you need a seat', said the officer to the small boy standing between adults on a crowded streetcar. Removing the shiny black cap perched on his right knee and handing it to the fellow officer sitting beside him, he reached for the lad, picked him up and placed him on his lap. Half to himself and half to those in earshot, he remarked that this was a cute little fellow. These words prompted the other officer, who was already troubled, to take a hard look at the boy and ask him, 'Are you an Aryan though?' The boy answered him truthfully and waited. 'Pity', said the officer holding him. He lifted the boy off his lap and placed him where he had been standing. The action was swift and smooth. While reclaiming his cap and again balancing it on his right knee, the SS man shook his head just perceptibly. Then both Germans stared straight ahead. To the boy it seemed as if he had suddenly become thin air. To the Viennese surrounding them he had, for all practical purposes, already ceased to exist." Not only was Vienna purged of its Jews, but Czech servants, Hungarian waiters, Balkan workers, Italian chefs no longer came there freely. After the *Anschluss*, tourists stayed away and international stars no longer stopped. More than the dissolution of its empire in the wake of World War I, for Vienna, what led to World War II was the end of an era.

Gertrud Bodenwieser left Vienna just after the *Anschluss*. Quite a few other refugees, severed from their habitual environment, could not go on with their work or did so only with difficulty, whereas Bodenwieser's productivity continued unabated. Could the reason have been that her work was not very Viennese? The one Bodenwieser piece this writer has seen (on video), *Demon Machine*, (as revived from Labanotation in 1990 for American dancers at the University of Washington in Seattle) might have been German Bauhaus choreography or repertory from the Russian Constructivist dance theater. Vienna, though, must have festered in Bodenwieser's being, for after the Nazi period and conclusion of World War II, she refused to return.

Notes

1. All the short stories quoted are from the set *Vienna, 1938* by the present author.
2. In 1887 nineteen artists broke away from the established art school (Künstlerhaus) and, under the leadership of Gustav Klimt, set up a group called the Secession. It gave its name to a building (which still exists), the exhibition hall for radical artists. The painters and dancers of the Secession were close friends of Gustav Mahler, Director of the Opera.
3. From the *Vienna* sonnet of *Music for the Tongue* by George Jackson, published in *Venture*: 60–61, 1961 (New York).
4. Formed in 1903 as a co-operative arts-and-crafts workshop, representing all aspects of design – jewellery, stamps, fabrics, furniture, cutlery. In revolting against ornateness of the mid-19th century, its members advocated the return to a simple style. Work took place in the building of the same name, which no longer exists for that purpose.

Bibliography

Barea, Isla. *Vienna.* Alfred A. Knopf; New York, NY, USA, 1966.

Baum, Vicki. *It Was All Quite Different.* Funk & Wagnalls Co.; New York, NY, USA, 1964.

Brooks-Shepherd, Gordon. *Austrian Odyssey.* Macmillan; London, UK, 1961.

Janick, Allan and Toulmin, Stephen. *Wittgenstein's Vienna.* Simon and Schuster; New York, NY, USA, 1973.

Morton, Frederic. *A Nervous Splendor – Vienna 1888/1889.* Little, Brown & Co.; Boston, MA, USA & Toronto, ON, Canada, 1980.

Morton, Frederic. *Thunder at Twilight – Vienna 1913/1914.* Charles Scribner's Sons/Macmillan; New York, NY, USA, 1989.

Schorske, Carl E. *Fin-de-Siècle Vienna – Politics and Culture.* Alfred A. Knopf; New York, NY, USA, 1980.

Wechsberg, Joseph. *The Vienna I Knew.* Doubleday; Garden City, NY, USA, 1979.

2

A DRIVING FORCE TOWARDS THE NEW. BODENWIESER – EXPONENT OF *AUSDRUCKSTANZ*

Gunhild Oberzaucher-Schüller

Gertrud Bodenwieser's oeuvre is typical of the *Ausdruckstanz* movement. She was one of the first exponents of this central European dance form. Her work, while possessing unique and distinctive features, is part of the overall movement, which has continued in various phases throughout the century. Firmly rooted, like other representatives of *Ausdruckstanz*, in a particular cultural environment and time, she is unlike most in creating less by intuition than by force of her intellect, education and an attitude of mind typical of a social stratum, the Jewish *haute bourgeoisie* of Europe. In contrast to almost all representatives of *Ausdruckstanz* (especially those of German origin), her work does not have its roots in a national context. The special, modified phenotype of her work derives less from her Viennese origins, being rather the expression of a supra-regional culture, which uses national elements as "local color". Gertrud Bodenwieser carries on the ideas of the greatest movement innovators, François Delsarte, Emile Jaques-Dalcroze, Rudolf von Laban, but, with a feel for the theater she takes from the new its extreme elements. Both as "creator-interpreter" and a group choreographer, she worked consciously with the tools of theatrical effect. For this reason, among others, she included classical ballet in her dance-training curriculum earlier than most other representatives of *Ausdruckstanz*. Bodenwieser was flexible, open to the artistic trends of her time: her dances were expressionist in the years of expressionism, later becoming more abstract and later yet acquiring fresh features, not least by virtue of the beauty of "her" dancers.[1] Bodenwieser was ultimately flexible enough to absorb the essence of a different cultural sphere, that of her new homeland, Australia, while leaving her personal stamp on it.

Confession and the ultimate expression of one's own self

It can safely be assumed that Gertrud Bodenwieser, who was born in 1890, observed the theater world and with it the dance world of her time with the greatest interest. Indeed, her gender and intelligence allowed her to become the ideal spokesperson for those American representatives of modern dance who, with the support of local (that is, Viennese) artists, were given the opportunity to display their art in the Vienna of the turn of the century. The now legendary appearances in Vienna of Loïe Fuller, Isadora Duncan, Maud Allan and Ruth St. Denis were not just key points in the creative path of the Americans, but also gave the emerging central Europeans the essential impulse to pursue their own path. There was much to learn from the Americans, who were also responsible for many initiatives: they discovered new venues for dance; they helped establish modern dance, which now took its place as an equal beside other art forms; they revolutionized the production and performance of dance; they helped to open up new subject areas for dance; they gave music a new status in relation to dance; they gained a new audience for dance from which the first generation of *Ausdruckstanz* was recruited; and finally, they played a decisive role in the process of women's self-discovery.[2]

The appearances by the Americans, which were warmly greeted, marked the beginning and the most important points in the first phase of the *Ausdruckstanz* movement; from the central European standpoint, this may be designated as the "observation" stage. Beginning in about 1900 and concluding around 1910, it was followed (even if it only became obvious with hindsight) by a framework extending over the 20th century that divides the central European *Ausdruckstanz* movement, and thus also the works of Gertrud Bodenwieser, into clearly separate phases.[3] After the observation phase came the "breaking-out" phase[4] from the early years of the second decade of the century until the beginning of the 1920s, followed by the phase of foundation laying, shaped by both pedagogical and economic factors; the subsequent creative stage of action appears to have come to an end before the Nazis seized power.[5] It was probably then (that is, before the effect of politics on the cultural scene) that the phase of exhaustion or at least of cultural stagnation began,[6] which was eventually followed, from the late 1970s, by the phase of reinvigoration that will probably come to its end with the new millennium.

The influence of the Americans on the work of Gertrud Bodenwieser, specifically its gender-specific aspects, may have been decisive. If instruction in dance under Carl Godlewski,[7] mentioned in all biographies of Bodenwieser, was part of the education of all young ladies, the decision to change her name (from Bondi to Bodenwieser[8]) was evidence of a determination to pursue her own artistic path, a path that upper-class young women could have followed only with great difficulty without the influence of the Americans.

The turmoil of the war years prevented public performances of the new dance[9] (and thus Bodenwieser's début), but could not interrupt the practical and theoretical examination of this artistic movement. On the contrary, for Bodenwieser the enforced pause allowed her ideas to mature, while the war also provided new subject matter.

Reflecting the imposed length of the "observation" stage, but also reflecting her temperament and intellect, Bodenwieser's "breaking-out" phase was less abrupt than that of other representatives of *Ausdruckstanz*. She saw herself at this time as closely bound up with the great spiritual current of the age, expressionism, to which she clearly subscribed, and her début as a dancer at the French Room[10] of the Vienna Konzerthaus, within the framework of the "New Union for Painting, Graphic and Plastic Art" exhibition, made a corresponding impact:

"…everything that the artist offered us was new, unquestionably new. We saw here for the first time what dance shows to advantage, what has been characteristic of the painting, poetry and music of the young for some time: the unconditional rejection of everything handed down and the honest search for new, purely personal expressive values…

In her technical execution the artist dispensed with all the existing dancer's impedimenta: step-based structure, illustrative mime, historical and ethnographic aids and links in movement and costume.

The principle of placing everything at the service of personal expression and of remaining completely free of any convention and tradition in the overall performance was visibly and consistently maintained. This was true throughout…

At any rate, in whatever direction this art may develop, one thing is certain: in Gertrud Bodenwieser we have made the acquaintance not only of a dancer completely modern in technique and concept with a rich individuality but also of one of the strongest dance temperaments of recent years, who in her original, dance-related, purely emotional way, is capable of producing the strongest impressions."[11]

This often quoted criticism by the most important Viennese dance reviewer of the time, Alphons Török, gives only a hint of the quality of the presentation, but also indicates, albeit indirectly, the influences that were decisive for Bodenwieser's first artistic phase. Like Grete Wiesenthal before her, Gertrud Bodenwieser also found in the fine arts the decisive stimulus to test her abilities. If the Vienna Secession movement was crucial for Wiesenthal, the same role was played for Bodenwieser by the artists of a later stylistic era. Among the painters closest to her at this time were Franz von Bayros, who collaborated on Bodenwieser's performances, and Felix Albrecht Harta, who was a member of the Hagenbund.[12]

In addition to the solo performances that resulted from her début, Bodenwieser also experimented with the dance duo form, her partners including Ernst Walt (in the early 1920s) and Curt Hagen (in the late 1920s) and worked from 1922 with a group. This work in particular brought to light the problems of training, to which she began consistently to devote herself in these early years.

Combining expression and technique

In the early 1920s, that is, at the inception of the expressionist phase of
Ausdruckstanz, Bodenwieser was already aware of the necessity for dance
training. (The main accent of performances at this early stage was placed
on presentation of the self and expression itself; physical or, indeed, dance
training was for the time being irrelevant.) While the phase of foundation-
laying still lay ahead, by 1921 Bodenwieser had succeeded in establishing
"artistic dance" as a subject at the Vienna State Academy of Music and the
Performing Arts.[13] At this early date Bodenwieser was distinguished from
almost all other representatives of *Ausdruckstanz* by her awareness that a
broad-based training was needed, in which classical ballet should have a
place, albeit a functional one. How progressive Bodenwieser was in this
respect is shown by the fact that, only a few years later, public discussion
on the inclusion of classical ballet in the curriculum of "modern" schools
split those attending the 1928 Essen dance congress into two camps. Mary
Wigman was the most prominent opponent, Kurt Jooss[14] the most important supporter. Hans Brandenburg, whose book *Der Moderne Tanz* (1913)
heralded the then nascent *Ausdruckstanz*[15] and who addressed the congress, looked back in 1931 at the Vienna Academy:

"The practice bar is there, as well as the ballet exercise, dancing on points. The
more moribund ballet is as a form and an absolute arbiter, the more it returns as
a separate element in the curriculum and as a technique. Indeed, the struggle
against ballet cannot be derived from the Western tradition, it was, like all
reforms, simply crisis, purification, expansion. A certain decline is no more than a
healthy response: Vienna is there to teach this and the Vienna Academy functions
seriously and without a mania for reform."[16]

Bodenwieser herself pursued the principle of a broadly-based
education and deepened her studies of Rudolf von Laban's books.[17] The
"Bodenwieser dance group" was formed from pupils of the State
Academy and of her own school, founded in 1922, which was an official
"Laban dance school". The group made its début in 1923 and continued
to exist, with a changing membership, until Bodenwieser's death.
Among the pupils who left Bodenwieser to pursue their own careers
were such names as Gertrud Kraus, Grete Gross, Hilde Holger, Gisa
Geert, Lisl Rinaldini, Trudl Dubsky, Erika Hanka and Cilli Wang.

Regarding contemporary man's world of feeling

On 15 December 1923 the *Brünner Tagesbote* reported on an evening of
dance presented by a Viennese dance group. The review, which probably

documents the first appearance by the Gertrud Bodenwieser dance group abroad, was both knowledgeable and informative. The reviewer, Dr. H. F., wrote:

"Should one call "dance" what Gertrud Bodenwieser shows us in the rhythmic interplay of groups and colors, what she herself conveys in her vocal expressive art, reminiscent of the manner of Rita Sacchetto?[18] The delightfully varied "scissor cut", ornamental pictures on a white surface, cut out as if with scissors, gracefully exaggerated twisting and entwinings of the hands, gliding and skipping along the canvas, always serving the surface effect, were equally original. *The Chinese Juggler* was wholly in the style of Sacchetto; on a high pedestal, wreathed in rising smoke … an idol comes to life, unreal, grotesque, lifting itself with convulsive movements from the underworld, straightening and sinking back. The art of movement is here, too, at the service of pictorial expression. And the same art is present in the shimmering *Caprice* (after Tchaikovsky), caught here in a gallant dance step. If Gertrud Bodenwieser is the lone herald of her art in these three numbers, she remains the center and guide of the individual dance groups which, as it were, visually express a multiplicity of feelings, the art of framing in a picture as in *Pious Way* or in the atmosphere of *Night*. A charming throng of youthful, gifted pupils is united here with her to form group pictures, always beautifully posed, that are kept in constant movement: Gisa Gehrt (sic), Hilde Holger, Hede Juer, Melitta Pfeiffer, Lisl Rinaldini and Marion Rischawy – dark and blonde, large and small in fine combination. Each possesses as her own the same play of hands, rhythmic firmness, elastic step. In the "Festive procession" the dance platform broadens out to become a stage, for which this production seems also intended. The dance group achieved effects on its own in three numbers: *Gnome*, *The Game of Knightly Struggle* – this in fact demanding a manly approach – and *Cry of Pain*. In each we saw line, self-confidence, precision and strict subordination to the guiding will of the leader, which can also be recognized in indirect effects. Gertrud Bodenwieser and her pupils were given a most friendly reception and received warm applause, in which the piano accompanist, Herr Arthur Kleiner, took a merited share".

Another quotation is equally informative and complements the first. It comes from no less a source than Hans Brandenburg, who on 31 May 1931 in the *Neueste Münchner Nachrichten* reported on a brief foray through the Viennese dance scene, noting that "only the new has the Viennese touch".[19] The author went on:

"Precisely because Vienna, historically and historico-geographically, is open to all influences, it is at once frontier and tradition. And since dance, too, is an historical fact, the schools reflect this. Affiliated to the State Academy of Music is a department of performing arts and music where Gertrud Bodenwieser holds the office and rank of professor and where Grete Gross also teaches. For the time being one sees here, far more than in Germany, female beauty preferentially, used consciously and with intent as a co-element in dance expression; and this beauty has the Viennese charm of subtle mixtures and varieties. Frau Bodenwieser spurns no inherited means of producing an effect through content, poetry or costume in the dance, all organized strictly as she requires and subordinated entirely to stage direction and thematic movement structure. When her group dances a machine dance, the fanatical demonstrator, the grim, demonic, hot and cold reality of a Vera Skoronel[20] are absent, rather the dance acquires something of the glitter of a theatrical fantasy. That is typical of Vienna, this theatrical element that is so important in art, for which there is a certain convention and which must be bound up with the technical and also with the external appearance of the external."

The first and second quotation, dancers and their program, the reviewer as arbiter – these are typical of the place and time.

The Brno report gives an especially vivid description of Bodenwieser's early, apparently very pictorial, choreographic style. The dominance of the leader is typical of the time, even when Bodenwieser attempts to integrate herself into the group, and it is also typical that the group is exclusively female in composition. The endeavor to include good-looking girls in the group, a fact that immediately caught Brandenburg's eye, is characteristic of Bodenwieser. Brandenburg's remark concerning the adoption of "inherited means of producing an effect" is also of interest.

Moulded by the spirit of the age

The focus of Bodenwieser's work now began to change. While the "music of the young" was always important, the realisation of "poetry" hand in hand with "kinetic accompaniment" gained increasing significance, especially in group works, until "dance drama" finally became the declared objective of her work.

At the same time Bodenwieser's larger group creations during the 1920s served as responses to intellectual and theatrical events in Vienna. This interplay with her artistic environment fundamentally distinguished Gertrud Bodenwieser from most other major representatives of *Ausdruckstanz*, who not merely worked outside the established theater but performed for themselves and within a small select circle of experts. In 1924 Bodenwieser produced the four-part dramatic dance sequence *The Forces of Life*, the second part of which, *Demon Machine*, set to the music of Lisa Maria Mayer, is one of her key creations. The music of the third part, *The Dance around the Golden Calf*, was created by Felix Petyrek. Bodenwieser's attempt in 1926 to encapsulate Oskar Kokoschka's *The Burning Bush*, which had been banned by the censor in 1913, in a 20-minute dance mystery to music by Alexander Tcherepnin at the Konzerthaus created a sensation. In the same year the music of Igor Stravinsky inspired her to create the caricature *Exotic Orchestra*. In *Rhythms of the Unconscious* (1928) to music by Egon Wellesz, Bodenwieser drew her inspiration from the teachings of Sigmund Freud, while in the second part of *Current and Counter-current* (1928) she again grappled with the theme of the mechanization of human life (the 'Ford System'). In 1931 in *The Great Hours* to the music of Tcherepnin she dealt with "the mystery of life".

Further evidence of Bodenwieser's roots in artistic Vienna was her work for the theater, in which the dance group assumed the function of a kinetic accompaniment or choir. This work also distinguished her essentially from the great representatives of *Ausdruckstanz* who, with few exceptions, declined to work for the theater since, in their view, this involved willingness to compromise.[21]

The most important theater works in which Bodenwieser and her group – for the most part functioning as kinetic chorus and involved in collaboration with often very well known directors – were *Franziska* by Frank Wedekind (1924) and *The Chalk Circle* by Klabund at the Raimundtheater in Vienna, both directed by Karlheinz Martin. They also participated in Fritz Kiesler's space stage experiment at the Konzerthaus (1924). For the first performance of the operetta *Paganini* by Franz Lehár at the Johann-Strauss Theater (1925) Bodenwieser choreographed two dances, which were performed by the group; the dance group was also involved in Hans Niedecken-Gebhard's 1927 production of Handel's *Hercules* at the Vienna Konzerthaus, for which Kurt Jooss created the choreography. In the same year Bodenwieser's group danced in the Vienna production of the *The Miracle* by Max Reinhardt at the Renz Circus (choreography for this production was by Ernst Matray).

At the beginning of the 1930s Bodenwieser finally turned to "dance drama". Drawing on the ambiguous symbolic content of mediaeval and religious subjects, the choreographer was able to weave into the action the atmosphere of topical political events. In 1930 she created *The Pilgrimage of Truth* and in 1936 *The Masks of Lucifer*, both to the music of Marcel Lorber, a long-time musical collaborator. During these years Bodenwieser also taught at the Reinhardt Seminar.[22]

Domestic success was now matched by international recognition. In 1926 Bodenwieser presented her group in Berlin, a stronghold of modern dance, and in 1929 the Bodenwieser group appeared in London, attracting wide interest. In 1931 it won the Grand Prix at the 'Olimpiade della Grazia'[23] in Florence and in 1932 gained a bronze medal at the 'Concours de Chorégraphie' in Paris. By 1938 the group had appeared in thirteen countries, in 1934 undertaking a major tour to Japan via Moscow. In the mid-1930s a second Bodenwieser group, which performed in New York and London, was formed to meet the company's many artistic commitments.

By the beginning of the 1930s Bodenwieser's status in the cultural life of Vienna was such that her participation in official occasions was indispensable. Mention should be made of appearances at major events, including the opening of the Vienna Festival Weeks in the Town Hall Square (1931), the spectacle *Vienna Remains Vienna* at the Vienna Stadium (1935) and the charity event *In the Rhythm of the Centuries* at Vienna's Hofburg (1938).

A driving force in a new and growing culture

If we referred originally to an organizing framework in connection with the *Ausdruckstanz* movement, which could be traced in the careers of leading dancers, we should now show some differences. A different creative path lay ahead for those creator-choreographers who were obliged to leave their homeland; two who came into this category were Gertrud Bodenwieser and Gertrud Kraus.[24]

While, after World War II, those dancers who had remained in their homeland sought to establish links with the period before World War I (an especially difficult aspiration since the change in aesthetics had not been produced by the cultural activities of the occupying powers alone), the emigrants had been able usually to initiate a very fruitful process of integration with the cultures of their new homelands, where they were the objects of dialogue among those active in the arts. Those who remained in Germany and Austria either persisted in the old ways or tried more or less to align themselves with the new aesthetics. Elsewhere something new came into being, as in the case of Gertrud Bodenwieser, growing from the combination of various cultural environments; it showed in the choice of subjects, choreographic language, dramaturgy and structure of dance dramas.

Shaken by the horrors of what she had experienced, Gertrud Bodenwieser placed herself on the side of the innocent and awarded them moral victory in her dance drama *Cain and Abel*, created in 1940 to the music of Lorber. In *O World*, to Tcherepnin's music, which dates from 1945, she warned of the vapid joys of victory and placed herself once again on the side of the suffering. In *Life of the Insects* after Karel Čapek, created in 1949 to music by Werner Baer, she opposed man's irrationality and inability to learn from history. Bodenwieser's last dance drama, *Errand into the Maze*, produced in 1954 to music by Gian Carlo Menotti, is ultimately dominated by scepticism: unable to find its way in the world, mankind unites in a solemn *danse macabre* and bemoans its fate.

After Gertrud Bodenwieser's death in 1959 modern creators of dance in Australia bemoaned their own fate and the end of an era and organized a recital in which her (available) oeuvre was staged. The reconstructions by Bettina Vernon and Evelyn Ippen of early dances, confirm in recent years the verdict passed then,[25] which refers simultaneously to the "impact of new ideas" and the "timeless value" of Bodenwieser's work, an opinion which, thanks to the reconstructions, a new generation of dance enthusiasts can endorse.

[Translated from the original German.]

Notes

1. In response to a question concerning her dance style, Bodenwieser replied (*Daily Telegraph*, 1 September 1939): "As yet I have given no name to it. Labels are always so incomplete and unsatisfactory. You call it, perhaps, impressionistic, expressionistic, futuristic, ultra-modern or whatever you like. But perhaps 'streamlined ballet' would express it best of all."
2. Cf. Gunhild Oberzaucher-Schüller, "Models and forerunners. The influence of the prime movers of American modern dance on the development of modern dance in Central Europe", in *Free Expressive Dance. A Central European movement in the first half of the 20th century*, Wilhelmshaven, 1992, pp. 347–366.
3. Although I do not believe that in the history of the arts there is continuous development, one period of art growing out of that which precedes it, this framework is far more than a mere aid to grasping the bewildering multiplicity of *Ausdruckstanz* performers and styles.
4. To characterize the almost furious determination of these choreographers to follow a new, different road with their dances, I have selected the term "breaking out".
5. See in particular the writings of Alfred Schlee who, in his journal *Schrifttanz*, referred openly to the stagnation of *Ausdruckstanz* as early as the beginning of the 1930s.
6. The futile search, at least among teachers, for a common denominator was the sign of a general crisis.
7. The dates of Bodenwieser's ballet instruction under Godlewski cannot be determined.
8. It has not been possible to verify the date of Bodenwieser's name change.
9. There were isolated performances during World War I (for example, Grete Wiesenthal in Vienna and Lucy Kieselhausen in Berlin).
10. "French Hall": presumably the French restaurant in the mezzanine of the Konzerthaus. At the time the hall was opened (1913) this had a balcony looking out on to an ice-skating rink. Today the premises house the dance school of Prof. Willy Franzl.
11. Alphons Török, "Dance evenings", in *Der Merker* 11, 1 June 1919.
12. The Hagenbund was an association of artists in Vienna formed at the turn of the century. Like most artists of the time, its members were close to dance. The Hagenbund made its premises at the Zedlitzhalle available for both dance classes and dance presentations. (See article by Alfred Oberzaucher and Gunhild Oberzaucher-Schüller p. 34.)

13. See Gabriele Renner, "Gertrud Bodenwieser", *Dissertation*, Vienna 1981, pp. 39–49. In the academic year 1920/21 Bodenwieser was already teaching "mime and dance" to drama and opera students of the Academy at the institute. From 1919 she conducted courses at the New Vienna Conservatory.

14. Kurt Jooss, together with Sigurd Leeder, had himself by this time studied ballet in Vienna under Irmgard Thomas.

15. Among the various, mutually hostile trends already in existence in this early (second) phase of *Ausdruckstanz*, each of which was philosophically based, Brandenburg represented the camp of Rudolf von Laban.

16. Hans Brandenburg, *Neueste Münchener Nachrichten*, 31 May 1931.

17. To what extent Bodenwieser actually studied under Laban is not known. She was seen at his summer school in Hamburg in 1923 and she certainly followed his method and principles.

18. Today Rita Sacchetto's decorative productions would be described as "living tableaux" rather than dance. She belonged to the group of "early individualists", who had performed before the work of Emile Jaques-Dalcroze (at Hellerau) or Rudolf von Laban (in Munich and Monte Verità). The "early individualists" also included Grete Wiesenthal, Sent M'ahesa, Clotilde von Derp and Alexander von Sacharoff.

19. In this connection Brandenburg noted that Rudolf von Laban "although an Austrian, (he) in fact has had no luck here". Brandenburg continued: "…but the journal *Schrifttanz*, edited by Alfred Schlee, which supports Laban's epoch-making invention, appears here".

20. The group constellation chosen in *Demon Machine* was, as photographs confirm, a set movement topos. Cf. photographs of *Demon Machine* with Vera Skoronel's drawings for *The Dance Game* and Max Terpis' *The Last Pierrot*. All the illustrations repeat the same "movement formula".

21. Jooss was one of the first important representatives to commit himself to a particular theater. The position changed after the end of World War II, when almost all the remaining active representatives of *Ausdruckstanz* worked in one form or another in the theater.

22. Bodenwieser taught at the Reinhardt Seminar in Vienna from 1932 to 1934.

23. In addition to the Bodenwieser dance group the ensembles of Elisabeth Duncan, Margaret Morris, Mary Wigman and Dorothee Günther also competed.

24. Gertrud Kraus, a pupil of Bodenwieser, was among the most striking personalities of Viennese modern dance. In 1935 she emigrated to Palestine, where she became a key figure in the dance movement in her new country.

25. Edward H. Pask, *Ballet in Australia. The Second Act 1940–1980*, Melbourne 1982, p. 70.

3

WHO WERE THE TEACHERS OF GERTRUD BODENWIESER? EDUCATIONAL OPPORTUNITIES AND DANCE ACTIVITY DURING THE PIONEERING PERIOD OF MODERN DANCE IN VIENNA

Alfred Oberzaucher and Gunhild Oberzaucher-Schüller

Delsartism and the teachings of Emile Jaques-Dalcroze and Rudolf von Laban form the intellectual and technical tools of *Ausdruckstanz*.[1] Depending on character and physical attributes, as well as the period of their formative years, the representatives of the central European modern dance movement subscribed to one, two or all three of these doctrines.[2]

Gertrud Bodenwieser named, retrospectively, it is true, Delsarte, Jaques-Dalcroze and Laban as the principal pillars of her artistic development. This presents the biographer with a headache since Bodenwieser's educational path is virtually unknown. The only relevant fact, that Bodenwieser studied classical ballet under Carl Godlewski,[3] proves on closer inspection to be an orally transmitted tradition that cannot be verified.[4]

Where and with whom did Gertrud Bodenwieser study?

A brief survey of educational opportunities during the pioneering period of modern dance in Vienna reveals what was available, but cannot give an answer to this question. Other questions, too, which must be considered in the light of contemporary practices, present themselves in connection with Bodenwieser's education. Did Bodenwieser, in fact, receive a thorough physical training?[5] Were attendance at a society dance school and ice-skating, the traditional pursuits that were the only forms of physical exercise possible for a young lady, Bodenwieser's "education"? What shape did Bodenwieser's formative years take? Did she learn from close analysis as an onlooker or, perhaps, from the detailed introductions to various "methods" that were taught in Vienna around 1910?[6] (Theoretical statements were characteristic of *Ausdruckstanz*. They were detailed and formulated consciously in order to contrast *Ausdruckstanz* with its self-declared, but silent, enemy, classical ballet.) It is, therefore, worth listing the dancers and groups who appeared in Vienna before Bodenwieser's début in 1919. We can safely assume that Bodenwieser, so far as her elevated social position permitted, took advantage of available opportunities. Since the training offered in Vienna and those who performed there in the first two decades of the 20th century were representative of other large cities important to the development of *Ausdruckstanz* (Berlin, Munich), listing them is of redoubled interest.

Where would the young Bodenwieser have found out what was happening around her, what could she have seen for herself and of what educational opportunities might she have been aware?

Modern dance was born in Vienna when Loïe Fuller appeared at the Etablissement Ronacher in 1898. This probably passed without note in the family of the then eight-year-old Bodenwieser, for her father, Johann Theodor Bondi, who was on the stock exchange, was probably not a typical habitué of the variety theater. Nor is it likely that he frequented the circle of artists belonging to the Secession, who had been deeply impressed by Fuller's appearance. We do not know whether the Bondi family attended the ballet at the Hofoper, the only place where dance was presented "seriously"; however, we do know that professional involvement with ballet and still more a ballet career were out of the question for a daughter of the Bondi family. Piano and ice-skating,[7] the latter sport also enjoyed in aristocratic circles, were acceptable.

In 1902 Fuller returned to Vienna. Her retinue included both the legendary Japanese actress Sada Yacco and the American modern dance pioneer Isadora Duncan, who performed in private at the Hotel Bristol and later, at the invitation of artists and through the mediation of Gustav Klimt, first at the Secession and then at the Künstlerhaus (both were exhibition halls). In 1903 Duncan gave her first theater performance, at the Carltheater, attracting, according to press reports, only the initiated. In the same year Maud Allan, the Canadian modern dancer, made her début in Vienna. She had many acquaintances in musical circles, which opened the doors of the Kleiner Musikvereinssaal to her for her performance. This unusual venue, reaching out to a new public, above all to women (and so to the women of the Bondi family), also fulfilled an educational function, since the "modern dancers" had no access to the great houses[8] and the "platforms" of the concert halls became the true home of *Ausdruckstanz*. Consequently, the performers were known as "platform dancers". In 1904 Duncan again performed at the Carltheater.

The year 1906 can be seen as marking the birth of Viennese modern solo dance, for it was this year that Gertrude Barrison, a dancer highly regarded principally in Viennese literary circles, took part in the inaugural programme of the Nachtlicht Cabaret.[9] Originally a variety dancer and enjoying a dubious renown in Europe as one of the five Barrison sisters, she was able not only to move into a more serious field but also to develop within her new career. Gertrude Barrison continued to play a significant role, both as a dancer and a teacher, in Viennese modern dance until the 1920s. It was in 1906 that Rita Sacchetto appeared at the Galerie Miethke, a venue to which the artist's decorative, pictorial dance style was superbly suited, while Maud Allan gave the first performance of her dance *Salome's Vision* at the Carltheater, a creation which she made world famous, but which represented a regression to the aesthetic of the variety theater. In 1907 Ruth St. Denis performed at the Ronacher. Her dancing was also an event that Vienna's artists were more likely to have noted than the social strata from which the coming generation of modern dance performers was drawn. Vienna's artists were in fact most aware of St. Denis' erotic brilliance, a quality that was probably its most outstanding feature at this stage of her career. In 1908 the Wiesenthal sisters (Grete, Elsa and Berta) made their début at Fledermaus, the cabaret of the Wiener Werkstätte. But Vienna was not the only city in which performances of these ballet-trained dancers became a synonym for modern dance *à la viennoise*. In the same year Ruth St. Denis gave the first performances of her solo dances *Nautch* and *Yogi* at the Ronacher and Olga Desmond appeared at the Apollo Theater, a traditional variety theater which was an appropriate home for her risqué poses. At the Kunstschau exhibition site the mime production[10] *The Birthday of the Infanta* (music by Franz Schreker, dance direction by Elsa Wiesenthal) was premiered, attracting a great deal of attention in Vienna and was certainly noted in Bodenwieser's circle. As a practising musician Bodenwieser, who was by then nineteen years old, was almost certainly aware of a "performance" in 1909, which formed a cornerstone of Jaques-Dalcroze's impact on Austria-Hungary: the master himself gave a lecture demonstration with a group of school pupils at the Musikverein.

With the opening of a school of Delsartism by Käthe Ulrich[11] in 1911, a new section of the public was given the opportunity to undertake physical education. Alphons Török, the chronicler[12] of the early Viennese modern dance scene, defined Delsartism in his book *Tanzabende*, published in 1918, as a method of:

"... training the body in an entirely physiological way to become a willing instrument for the natural physical expression of spiritual events ... The method, which is most widespread in America, soon found able representatives in Germany as well, including Elisabeth Duncan, Hade Kallmeyer and Dr. Bess Mensendieck.[13] Whereas for the first two, gymnastic instruction is designed more with a view to later artistic expressiveness, the Mensendieck system lays greater stress on the medical aspect. Participation in a course of this kind is now an urgent necessity for all aspiring dancers."[14]

A 1911 production at the Hofoper of *The Veil of Pierrette* (libretto by Arthur Schnitzler, music by Ernst von Dohnányi, Harlequin mimed by Carl Godlewski) was regarded as a work blazing a new trail, and must also have been noted in the Bondi household.

In 1912 a branch of the Hellerau school opened in Vienna under the direction of Eduard Favre and Suzanne Perrottet. This gave the opportunity for physical exercise to a wide group of piano students (girls and women). In 1918 Alphons Török reported on the significance of rhythmic gymnastics for contemporary modern dance:

"Originally intended only to fill obvious gaps in our musical education, it offers the teacher through the consistently developed idea of physical realization of particular, physically experienced musical elements, rhythm, dynamics and agogics, the opportunity of observing the growing receptiveness of pupils; it also makes it possible to eliminate nervous inhibitions by means of a series of exercises and to achieve a spontaneous rendering of what is heard."[15]

The year 1912 also saw the opening by Elsa and Berta Wiesenthal of a school, while Grete Wiesenthal made her first appearance as a soloist at the Apollo Theater after separating from her sisters. Adorée Villany appeared the same year, her risqué nude dance (presented under the euphemism of "naturalness") more suited to the variety theater. At the Rotunde in 1912, Vienna saw a series of performances of Max Reinhardt's legendary production, *The Miracle,* a theatrical event of which Gertrud Bodenwieser would certainly have known. Reinhardt returned in the following year with his renowned production of *Sumurûn* (libretto by Friedrich Freksa, music by Victor Hollaender), which was produced in collaboration with Grete Wiesenthal at the Lustspieltheater. For observers of Viennese modern dance the year 1913 was especially eventful: the Jaques-Dalcroze Association and the "Association for Rhythmic Gymnastics" were founded and, during its second visit to Vienna, the Ballets Russes presented such revolutionary works as *Petrushka* and *L'après-midi d'un Faune.*[16] No less important, however, was a new production, at the Hofoper, of *Tannhäuser*, in which the Venusberg bacchanalia was choreographed by Suzanne Perrottet. The visit of Ellen Tels[17] and her ensemble to the Apollo Theater, marking the first appearance by a modern dance group in Vienna, attracted wide attention. Grete Wiesenthal also returned to the Apollo and 1913 saw Lucy Kieselhausen's début.

In 1914 the influence of Jaques-Dalcroze's teaching spread and Gertrud Wiesenthal, yet another Wiesenthal sister and a graduate of

Hellerau, joined the teaching staff of the Vienna Academy of Music and the Performing Arts. A further performance of rhythmic gymnastics under Jaques-Dalcroze's direction at the Musikvereinssaal consolidated his influence. The appearance by Clotilde von Derp and Alexander von Sacharoff at the Apollo Theater marked the first performance by a modern dance couple in Vienna. While the war year 1915 appears to have lacked any events noteworthy in the development of modern dance, in 1916 Grete Wiesenthal, partnered by Carl Godlewski, danced at the Musikverein, a hall which subsequently saw performances by Rita Sacchetto and, later, Käthe Ulrich in a "rhythmic-plastic expressive evening". 1916, however, was also marked by a special event. At the Theater an der Wien Ernst Freund (Ferand)[18] produced the mime *The Prodigal Son* (music by André Wormser) and also trained the diva Betty Fischer and the soubrette Louise Kartousch, two stars of Viennese operetta, who were appearing at the theater. The year 1917 too was eventful as far as dance was concerned. In addition to already familiar material, Käthe Ulrich again presented a performance of Delsartism, while Sent M'ahesa and Ellen Petz appeared for the first time in Vienna.

When the restrictions brought by war were removed at last, there was a flood of dance productions. We shall mention only those dancers whose reputations have survived. Dance performances were given by Ellen Petz, Gertrude Barrison, Grete Wiesenthal, Lucy Kieselhausen, Sent M'ahesa, Ronny Johansson,[19] Olga Desmond and Rita Sacchetto among others. There were also performances by the dance couple Lo Hesse and Joachim von Seewitz, and by three Wiesenthal sisters (Elsa and Berta were now joined by Marta) and the Braun sisters, Jeanne, Leonie and Lili, pupils of Jaques-Dalcroze, who presented a dance evening at the Konzerthaus. The Association for Rhythmic Gymnastics in Vienna presented *Performances in Rhythmic Gymnastics* in which dancers from Vienna, Budapest, Prague, Brno, Graz and Basel appeared. (Among those involved who later became known as dancers or teachers were Margarete Kallab from Brno, who was Rosalia Chladek's teacher, and Olga Szentpál from Budapest.)

As early as 1918 Török published what amounted to a summing up:

"Starting with the Wiesenthals who took the waltz and expanded it to become a symbol of individual joy in dance – and epitomised the personality dance for us – through to the mime performances, rooted in the old school, of Kieselhausen, Cerri[20] and Petz, the Barrison style, which did justice to old as well as new stylistic modes and the arts and crafts, the ethnographic direction of Sent M'ahesa, up to the self-taught, thoroughly modern expressive forms of a Desmond, a Johansson or a Seewitz, through all these various manifestations we see the struggle for a modern form of expression revealing the personality."[21]

The year 1919 saw further débuts: in addition to the "Orchestral Society" (a permanent Budapest group, directed by Dr. Valéria Dienes, which was aligned with Raymond Duncan), Loe (later Maria) Ley[22] and Elsie Altmann[23] also made their first appearances in Vienna. The début of Gertrud Bodenwieser, however, drew most attention. Her appearance within the framework of an exhibition at the Vienna Konzerthaus was unusual and betrayed her relationship to the fine arts. Her oft-quoted closeness to the Hagenbund association of artists may have been mediated by Grete Bieberbach (1885–1968), a pupil of Jaques-Dalcroze. Viennese-born, Bieberbach was initially a concert pianist. After meeting Jaques-Dalcroze in Geneva, she became Favre's assistant in the "Association for Rhythmic Gymnastics", which gave performances at the Hagenbund. If Bodenwieser attended classes organised by the association, she could have come into contact with the Hagenbund.[24]

In the middle of his report on Bodenwieser's début Alphons Török writes:

"The artist's programme, comprising a mere six items, mirrored in its very structure the scope and nature of what was offered: linearity, en profile, projected on to the level of her art (Reinhold's *Silhouette*). Its character expanded to symbolize the modern psyche, developing with all its complicated, absurd stirrings and its spontaneous changes of mood (stimulus, hysteria), the eternal song of demon woman and of 'Eros, the all-conquering in conflict' in a completely original light (Rubinstein, *Spanish Dance*, and Debussy, *Cakewalk*) and finally strange, grotesque-burlesque refractions in expressions of happiness and high spirits (Reinhold, *Burletta* and Rachmaninov, *Groteske*)."[25]

As well as these solo evenings, the agenda for that year also included Dalcroze and Delsarte performances. A further major event in the already firmly established Vienna modern dance scene was the appearance by Ellen Tels and her ensemble, now resident in Vienna.

Bodenwieser's 1919 début in private seems to have been a dress rehearsal for her first public performance, which finally took place in 1920 in the large auditorium of the Konzerthaus[26] in an evening *Dances-Grotesque*. The six solo numbers she had performed in 1919 were supplemented by the following dances: *Egyptian Impression* (music by Cyril Scott), *Faun's Jest* (music by Ede Poldini) and *Pas de Caractère* (music by Alexander Glazunov). The costume designs were again by Franz von Bayros.

The dancer's first successes are reflected in an undated letter from Bodenwieser to Hermann Bahr, in which she requested his assistance. She describes herself in the following way: "I am a dancer and have found a new style in my art."[27] Bahr obviously responded to her request, for no less a figure than Max Reinhardt placed his Berliner Kammerspiele at Bodenwieser's disposal.

The dancer's Berlin début took place on 2 May 1920 at a matinée.[28] Bodenwieser thus became one of the first *Ausdruckstanz* performers to appear after the war in Berlin under Reinhardt's auspices.[29]

The midday edition of the *Berliner Zeitung* of 5 May 1920 contained the following notice:

"Gertrud Bodenwieser presents dances at the Kammerspiele that do not deny their intelligent origins. They do not spring from a light-hearted sensuality but from pure reflection and would be inconceivable without quite definite models. These patterns are not slavishly imitated – for that to happen Miss Bodenwieser contributes too much invention and temperament – but her dependence on Sent M'ahesa in her Egyptian impression and Valeska Gert in her Spanish dance is unmistakable. She is closer to Sent M'ahesa than to Gert, probably because her parody still lacks a grain of recklessness... Miss Bodenwieser – one could certainly lay a wager that she has passed her 'Matura'[school leaving examination] – is eloquent in the vivid play of her hands, finding in this surprising and fresh nuances."

Bodenwieser's subsequent artistic career is well known.

[Translated from the original German.]

Notes

1. We cannot discuss here the differing approaches underlying the methods of these theorists and shall note only that Delsarte and Jaques-Dalcroze were originally concerned with movement, not dance. It should be stressed that, especially in the first two decades of the 20th century, at least three attempts were made to achieve an alignment with dance: (a) by the fine arts: these "dancers" appealed principally to Delsartism, which was taught in schools as early as 1910, (b) by musicians: the appeal here was made to Jaques-Dalcroze, whose widespread impact began to be felt from the beginning of the second decade of this century, and (c) chronologically last, by dancers: appealing to Rudolf von Laban, who was active from 1910, but whose immense impact was first felt only after his period at Monte Verità.
2. Or to the pupils of the three theorists.
3. Carl Godlewski (1862–1942), the first mime artist of the Hofoper, was originally a circus performer but had also studied in St Petersburg with Alfred Bekefi. He played an important role in the new genre of mime and choreographed, among other works, *The Snowman* (music by Erich Wolfgang Korngold, 1910) for the Vienna Hofoper. In 1919 he was ballet master of the Staatsoper. From about 1907 he had his own school in Vienna (4th District, Kleinschmidgasse), which Bodenwieser attended. Godlewski was regarded as open-minded with respect to the new and in 1907 expressed the following views in an interview

with *Die Zeit* concerning performances by American dancers in Vienna: "It is scarcely possible to predict whether they will bring about a reform of the ballet... Reform of the ballet which, I believe, has already begun, is presently focused on character dancing." Prophetic words, if one recalls that it was with character dancing and character dancers that the Ballets Russes achieved its greatest successes. In this respect one cannot but wonder what modern dance performers had in mind when they claimed that ballet was dead. The performances of the Ballets Russes in the great theater centers of Germany date from the years immediately before World War I.

4. Of interest in this connection is a comment made to the authors by Carl Raimund junior. Bodenwieser had intended to attend the ballet school of his father, Carl Raimund senior, but was rejected in view of her age. According to his son, Raimund senior was probably also motivated by anger at the hostile attitude towards classical ballet then shown by exponents of *Ausdruckstanz*. From this we may suspect that Bodenwieser's intention to study ballet remained alive far later than is generally assumed, that is until the end of the second decade or the beginning of the third decade of this century, and that she went to Godlewski after her "rebuff" by Raimund.

5. Only her participation in a summer course under Rudolf von Laban in 1923 has been verified.

6. In this connection we may refer to another Viennese artist whose career was very similar to that of Bodenwieser. The educational history of Margalit Ornstein (born Grete Oppenheimer) 1888–1973 is also unknown. Two years older than Bodenwieser, she could have followed an entirely similar path. As early as 1922 she went to Palestine as the first representative of central European *Ausdruckstanz* and taught "Plastic Gymnastics and Rhythmic Exercises" there. Like Bodenwieser she declared her support for Jaques-Dalcroze, Laban and Mensendieck. Both her daughters, Jehudit and Shoshana, played an important role in Israeli modern dance as dancers and teachers, studying initially with their mother and later in Vienna (with Bodenwieser) and Berlin.

7. The Vienna ice-skating association, which was founded in 1867, was located from 1901 on part of the land on which the Konzerthaus was built. The Hall, erected in 1913, was Bodenwieser's domain from 1919 to 1938. She made her début there, appeared regularly until 1936, taught in the private school she opened in the basement (known, following Rudolf von Laban, as the "School for Movement Art") and was a member of the teaching staff of the State Academy, which was housed in a part of the complex, from 1920 to 1938. In this context we may note that Louis Horst studied at the Konzerthaus during his stay in Vienna in 1925.

8. Both Isadora Duncan and her American contemporary Ruth St. Denis appeared at opera houses in Berlin. Their requests to perform at the Hofoper were declined, no reasons being given.

9. The reference is to a new, artistically demanding form of cabaret shaped by contemporary arts. Among the best-known cabarets of this type was Fledermaus, where the Wiesenthal sisters made their début.

10. A genre that emerged around the turn of the century in connection with a new conception of dance. Mime productions were for the most part created by well-known authors and composers. Their plots were conveyed solely by movements of every part of the body.
11. Käthe Ulrich studied under Hade Kallmeyer, a pupil of Genevieve Stebbins.
12. Török wrote in *Der Merker* from 1917 to 1921. He was preceded in his post as reviewer by Paul Czinner, later a director, and succeeded by Victor Junk.
13. The teaching of Bess Mensendieck (propagated in Vienna by Philine Lahr, whose school was in the immediate vicinity of the Bondis' home) became so widespread in central Europe that not only were followers of Mensendieck known as "Mensendieckers" (like "Labaners"), but also the verb "mensendiecken" was created; this verb was included among foreign words listed in *Duden*.
14. Alphons Török, *Tanzabende*, Vienna 1918, pp. 31–32.
15. *Ibid.*, p. 30.
16. The Vienna performances of the Ballets Russes were the subject of newspaper commentaries by Viennese (classical) dancers and choreographers. The only unambiguously positive response to the works presented by the Russians was written by Carl Godlewski.
17. Ellen Tels: see Elisabeth Suritz, "The 'plastic' and 'rhythmic-plastic' dance in Russia in the 1910s and 1920s", in *Free Expressive Dance. A Central European movement in the first half of the 20th century*, ed. Gunhild Oberzaucher-Schüller, Wilhelmshaven 1992, pp. 405–420.
18. Ernst Ferand-Freund (as he later called himself) was a pupil of Jaques-Dalcroze who, with Christine Baer-Frissell and Valeria Kratina, directed the Hellerau school from 1920. In 1925 the school moved to Laxenburg near Vienna. This was the school attended by Edwin Denby, the American critic and writer on dance.
19. Johansson was born in Sweden and studied Delsartism in Stockholm. She became a well-known solo dancer in central Europe and ultimately moved to America. From 1929 she taught with Elsa Findlay in New York. The latter, an Englishwoman, had studied under Jaques-Dalcroze at Hellerau and was the first representative of rhythmic gymnastics to teach at Denishawn, the school set up by Ruth St. Denis and Ted Shawn.
20. Noting the success of the modern dance exponents, ballet dancers, too, began to present solo dance evenings. One such dancer was Cäcilie Cerri, prima ballerina of the Hofoper and subsequently the Staatsoper, between 1907 and 1921.
21. Alphons Török, *Tanzabende*, Vienna 1918, p. 29.
22. Ley married Erwin Piscator and was also active in his New York actors' studio.
23. Altmann, briefly married to the Viennese architect Adolf Loos, changed genre, establishing herself as a leading dance soubrette in 1924 with the role of Lisa in Emmerich Kalmán's *Countess Maritza*.
24. Grete Wiesenthal opened her school at the Hagenbund (Zedlitzgasse) in 1927.
25. The beginning and conclusion of Török's critique is quoted on page 21 in the article by Gunhild Oberzaucher-Schüller.

26. The great auditorium of the Konzerthaus held 2030. Although we cannot establish now how many tickets were sold, Bodenwieser might well have hired one of the smaller halls if she did not anticipate a large audience.

27. Reprinted in *Dance. The 20th Century in Vienna*, exhibition catalogue, Vienna 1979, p. 104. The letter continues: "... (I) am writing to you as the great helper of youth, the sponsor of all those who are struggling and fighting for something new, with the request not to refuse me your favor. I am going to Berlin, where I am a complete stranger and I should like to ask you most urgently for a recommendation to the dance expert there, Oscar Bie, or to anyone else who could give me a little help there in my efforts."

28. We should like to thank Rolf Iden of Berlin, who searched the Berlin press for notices of Bodenwieser's matinée.

29. Bodenwieser certainly took advantage of the city's cultural opportunities during her Berlin sojourn. She could have attended a performance of Frank Wedekind's *Franziska* at the Tribüne, a play that was of significance to her later work in Vienna.

4

GERTRUD BODENWIESER:
DANCE FOR THE THEATER

Jarmila Weissenböck

Gertrud Bodenwieser was responsible for the choreography of various theatrical productions. The significance of these works must in no way be underestimated as far as the Viennese expressionist theater of the 1920s is concerned. It is indeed Gertrud Bodenwieser herself, who in her own words acknowledges that expressionism was both the artistic form and language of her time: "'Gracefulness', although always in days gone by emphasised and required as an essential factor towards the impact of a dance, is perceived by me with its stiffness and refinement as a biased limitation of the concept of beauty. Nor do I consider it worth striving for the principle of controlling movements according to the familiar notions of ancient times, as portrayed by illustrations, because it is no longer in tune with the spirit of our times. I would much prefer to ensure that the whole vast area of human feeling should be accessible to free expressive dance, especially the entire ambit of modern man's emotions … conflict, passion, unrestrained, intensified life experience, but I also wish to see demonstrated chaos, fear, degeneracy in the dances without consideration for the aesthetic line, and maybe for that very reason to show them with even more forceful momentum. I have recognised Rodin's dictum, namely that beauty is character and expression, as a waymark for my work. And therefore I endeavor to bring dance into the closest relationship to this great intellectual movement, expressionism, in which I firmly believe."[1]

It is from this artistic standpoint that the undermentioned choreographies must be considered: based on personal experience, emanating from the spirit of the times together with a keen sensibility, a sure sense of style and an up-to-date approach.

Historical background

At the beginning of the 20th century the revolutionary changes in Russian stage productions by Alexander Tairoff and Wsewolod Meyerhold, as well as the newly emergent concept of movement, together with the innovative solutions to the spatial problem on stage by Edward Gordon Craig and Adolphe Appia had paved the way for the future. This was relevant also for Leopold Jessners's handling of group and crowd scenes on the Berlin stage of the 1920s. It was this kind of group movement, entirely integrated into the production, as seen in the chorus and the 'extras' that led almost inevitably to the choreographic solutions for dancers. This 'chorus of movement' – since the 1920s an aspect of Rudolf von Laban's artistic creativity – can be seen as the mainstay of the plot, as well as a reflection or continuation and interpretation of the action, and/or yet again of the psychological state and innermost emotions of the protagonists.

Max Reinhardt

In 1909 Max Reinhardt, one of the first 'modern' producers, included a dancer, Grete Wiesenthal, as a fairy in his new production of *Midsummer Night's Dream* in Munich's Künstlertheater. The following year at the Berliner Kammerspielen in his production of *Sumurûn*, again with Grete Wiesenthal, he advanced the development of the increasing importance of choreography, in a mime.

It was also a mime which was the only collaboration between Bodenwieser and Reinhardt: *Das Mirakel* (*The Miracle*) in the latter's 1927 Viennese production in the Renz Circus. For Ernst Matray's creation of the choreography Gertrud Bodenwieser made available for Max Reinhardt those of her dancers most experienced in modern, expressive dance.

Gertrud Bodenwieser–Friedrich Rosenthal

Gertrud Bodenwieser, who was already twenty-nine years old when she gave her first solo performance in 1919, was well acquainted with this European development of bringing theater and expressionist dance together. This acquaintance came first out of personal interest, but later also through her husband Friedrich Rosenthal, dramaturge, producer (from 1913 at the Volkstheater, from 1932 onwards at the Burgtheater) and writer on artistic topics, whom she married in 1920. Friedrich Rosenthal had worked as assistant producer on Max Reinhardt's 1913 production of *The Miracle* at the Vienna Volksoper. In the summer of the same year he visited Hellerau near Dresden and there had witnessed Emile Jaques-Dalcroze's *Orpheus* which virtually had become part of dance history. It was for this production that Adolphe Appia had designed a purpose-built stepped stage. For Rosenthal it was a production "which took place on a very simple stage, but up to a point it was a decisive event and a beginning, as it established that decorative and relief-like principle based on modern crowd movement, which later formed the basis of every modern *Orpheus* production."[2] That summer's experiences had made a deep impression on Rosenthal, and were not without influence on his later productions. We now know of the artistic collaboration between Bodenwieser and Rosenthal, and we also realise that Gertrud Bodenwieser was fully *au fait* with all cultural events and Rosenthal's work. We can take for granted her detailed knowledge of the development of the various movements and trends in European theater as a foundation of her creative work, not only in connection with the spoken theater: "It happens more and more that dance is being brought into drama. However not, as in the past, occasionally as a dance scene within the drama, but as an accompaniment of movement throughout the whole play, as an arabesque completely integrated into the acts of the drama. The Russian theater was the first to give way to this strong desire for scenic movement; itself a product of the revolution, it led the way. We witness already the impact of the spoken word being heightened through movement, grouping and striking changes in the levels of the scenic structure. Western theater follows the lead, hesitatingly, and yet as if by an inner compulsion. The rigidity of a scene is broken up, the effects flowing from the movements taken into account and full use is made of dance, no longer now as a mere interlude or a 'filler', on the contrary it is interwoven with the drama, strengthening and intensifying it at the same time: a means of expression of the dramatic action, just as much as the words, the costumes and the scenery."[3]

Der Verschwender (The Spendthrift)

Gertrud Bodenwieser's collaboration with Friedrich Rosenthal was given its only artistic expression in the première of the new production of Ferdinand Raimund's *Der Verschwender* at Vienna's Volkstheater on 3 November 1923.

Gertrud Bodenwieser saw her task as choreographer within the framework of Friedrich Rosenthal's production as follows: "It was a case of instilling into the formality of the old Viennese type of dance scenes of fairies and cupids, a fantasy strong in expression by means of dance movements in tune with today's idea of the character of such an atmosphere. It concerned mainly the closing scenes of Act 1, Cheristane's farewell to Flottwell, in which the traditional magic devices of the old-time Viennese fairy-plays were usually displayed. The tragi-romantic character of this scene was lost and was no longer relevant in this form for today's sensibilities. The dramatic rhythm of this scene and its sombre descriptive music were now expressed and complemented by a vividness, just as great, of cupids dressed in dignified costumes, expressed in economical and at the same time sensitive movements."[4]

Although nowadays we cannot quite imagine such an interpretation, especially of a Raimund fairytale-play, it is, nevertheless, completely in the spirit of historical development to stage even a traditional Viennese play in a way tending towards an expressive modern style.

In the scene described by Bodenwieser herself, as indeed in later choreographies without a plot, such as *Relief*, 1928, or *Die Kugel*, 1931, the graphic vividness of her animated dancers (as well as the help of the title), and possibly also connected with Rosenthal's impressions of the 1913 *Orpheus* in Hellerau, plays a significant role.

The reasons that there were no further Bodenwieser / Rosenthal collaborations can be found not only in the fact that Rosenthal had left the Volkstheater for good by 1926 and was not active again as producer until 1932 at the Burgtheater, but also because of the Bodenwieser company's extremely full schedules, especially foreign tours (at times three separate companies were touring Europe) and also because of Gertrud Bodenwieser's extensive teaching activity: at the Academy, the Reinhardt Seminar, and her private school at the Konzerthaus. Loli Petri, student and dancer in the Bodenwieser company and, later on, Bodenwieser's deputy at the Academy, worked as a choreographer at the Burgtheater from 1936–1938. There, in productions by Rosenthal and Ernst Waniek she continued, in the spirit of Bodenwieser, the legacy of choreographic work for the spoken drama.

Franziska

Bodenwieser's best-known choreography for the theater was for *Franziska* in December 1924.

In the autumn of that year Friedrich Kiesler had introduced his sensational space stage project at the Vienna Konzerthaus; it was no surprise that Gertrud Bodenwieser and her company devoted an evening to this theatrical experiment. On 20 December, a mere month and a half after the discontinuance of the project, Karlheinz Martin had his production of Frank Wedekind's *Franziska* premiered at the Raimundtheater. Karlheinz Martin, having already tried one production on Kiesler's stage structure, now adapted it to the Raimundtheater's proscenium stage and with this compromise solution achieved a considerably greater and immediate success than Friedrich Kiesler with his uncompromising, totally innovative space stage. Karlheinz Martin was in charge of the production on this stage, which was at once described by the critics as a space stage, and Gertrud Bodenwieser, having had, of course, previous experience with Kiesler's stage structure, was engaged as choreographer. Bodenwieser regarded her work for *Franziska* in complete contrast to the problems of Raimund's *Der Verschwender*: "Here it was a case of even transcending the demonic, passionate and swirling rhythm of that production, depicted in garish colors, by means of dances. On two occasions it was necessary for the dancers to intervene in this way through an extra special intensity: once, when in the wine-bar scene, we see Franziska moving around in the bacchanalian surroundings to which Veit Kunz had introduced her; and then again in the 'theater' scene, when the Chorus of the Shades, dancing to the spoken lines by Franziska, here appearing as actress in the scene of the play within the play. The dancers as Chorus of the Shades move across and off the stage, only to rush on again, this time in frenzied madness, at the very moment of Veit Kunz's realization that he has been betrayed and taunted by Franziska and Ralph, her brutish partner, the dancers, singly and all of them together, portraying an unequivocal symbol of emancipated womanhood."[5]

Alfred Polgar especially rated the stage structure very highly, which "...forces the performers to move freely. Thus acting, like light, spreads wave-like in all directions. The space stage allows for exceptionally lively and varied mass groupings... scorn and shame as opposed to the emotional appeal of the traditional and established theater."[6]

The outstanding success of this production resulted in an invitation from Berlin in the spring of 1925, including Gertrud Bodenwieser and her company. Tilla Durieux created the title role, as she had done in Vienna.

Der Kreidekreis (The Chalk Circle)

It was undoubtedly the great success of *Franziska* that led to further collaboration with Karlheinz Martin. Klabund's *Kreidekreis* was premiered on 16 September 1925 in the Raimundtheater. This time the stage was set up with practicable raised platforms, enabling the desired scene changes, which were carried out by the dancers as part of the overall choreography, to take place on the open stage.

This time Gertrud Bodenwieser considered her choreographic work as a further and third variation of empathy of dance with drama. "This time the dancers created a chorus, completely in keeping with classical drama, accompanying all the actions, however not as solemnly as in Greek tragedy, but parodistically in a double sense: parodying the action as well as its own choric individuality.

Dancers were at the beginning and end of the drama, they formed the prologue, the accompanying action and the epilogue. They were never off the stage; they had to carry out all ornamental transformations and provide all stage props, of course, always through dance-like movements. Thus they were described by the producer both as dancers and servants of the drama."[7]

But however much enthusiasm people had shown at the *Franziska* collaboration of Karlheinz Martin and Gertrud Bodenwieser, and however successful this production had been at the Berlin guest performance, this time, alas, it did not find the expected favor. Critical voices accused Karlheinz Martin of transforming "everything he touched into a drama of ecstasy, as he understands it… The stage is full of color, ribbons, garlands and surprises, and since Tairoff, a company of charming chorus girls on such an evening would dance and dance until their legs (albeit on this occasion for the most part covered) could dance no more.

Without exception they are symbolic maidens: at times women of easy virtue, at others, servants, but now and then also portraying forces of nature. But what I considered most deplorable was that the desolation and loneliness of the snow-storm scene was hideously enlivened by dancing girls."[8]

Faust

After Friedrich Rosenthal's departure from the Volkstheater in 1926, there was a collaboration with Rudolf Beer on a production of Goethe's *Faust*. The première took place on 10 September. Both parts one and two of the drama were produced in a five-hour performance, praised by the critics, especially Alfred Polgar, as a great success. Paul Mederow, in charge of the theatrical production, was the Faust and Otto Schmöle Mephistopheles. The production was said to have been fully 'integrated';[9] this was due to Gertrud Bodenwieser's experience in this genre, the clever and effective use of her dancers in mass scenes and the witches' scenes of the Classical Walpurgis Night, and especially also in *Faust*, Part II.

Through the work with her dancers in the spoken theater a new perspective opened up for Gertrud Bodenwieser: "The relationship between the art of movement and that of the spoken word",[10] if the dancers "move only according to the melody of the word without any further musical support. Our attention is drawn with a much sharper focus to the rhythmic construction of speech, indeed to the most subtle timbre and shade of the spoken word. The infinite beauty and richness of the art of speaking are felt all the more deeply and revealingly."[11] A further development of this trend could be seen in the choreographic guidance of the classical choruses of Rosalia Chladek's Company Hellerau-Laxenburg in the 1930s in Syracuse.

Klassische Walpurgisnacht im neuen „Faust" am Deutschen Volkstheater

Photo Willinger

Mephisto (Schmölle) und die thessalischen Hexen (die Gruppe Bodenwieser)

3 Classical Walpurgis Night from *Faust*, choreographed by Bodenwieser in 1926. Mephisto and the Thessalian witches. Photo: Willinger.

4 Emmy Taussig expresses "Intrigue" in the trilogy *The Masks of Lucifer* in which Satan appears in succession as "Intrigue", "Terror" and "Hate". Choreographed before Hitler invaded Austria, 1936.

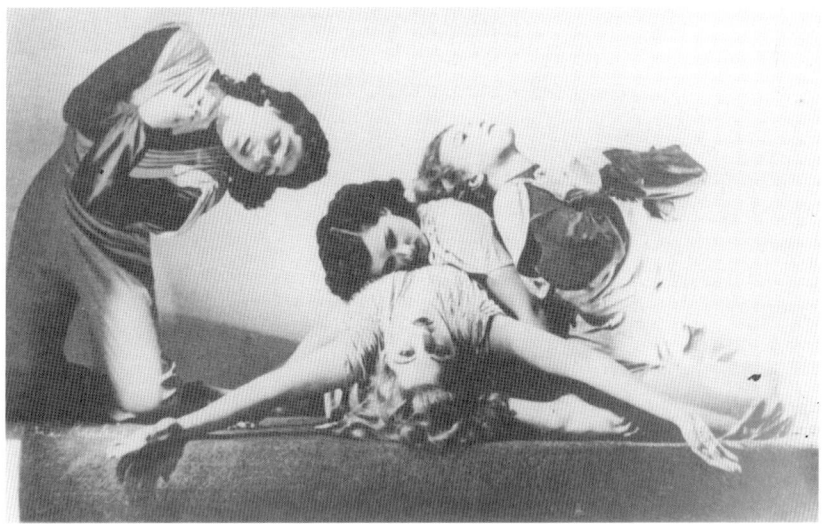

5 *The Masks of Lucifer*. "Terror", Katja Georgieva, Emmi Steininger, Bettina Vernon, Melitta Melser. Photo: Nöel Rubie, Sydney 1940.

6 *The Masks of Lucifer*. "Hate". From a press cutting circa 1940.

7 *Errand into the Maze*. From the program of a performance "Tribute to Gertrud Bodenwieser", Conservatorium of Music, 28 September 1960, Sydney.

Dance Drama

The result of Gertrud Bodenwieser's analysis of her creative work was "that the link between the expressiveness of the dancer and that of the actor means for us a valuable enrichment, that the opportunities for dance within the spoken drama are unlimited, presenting a host of new problems, which in turn offer fresh opportunities for work and development."[12]

Bodenwieser herself, however, made no use of these opportunities. She decided, for whatever reason, on a different form of dance exposition of language, namely with literature. Her language is that of dance interpretation of dramatic contents, the Dance – grown out of her experiences, orientated towards her forerunners Delsarte, Mensendieck, Jaques-Dalcroze and Laban. One of Bodenwieser's paths led to Dance Drama: *The Masks of Lucifer*, first produced in Vienna in 1936. After her emigration to Australia there followed: *Cain and Abel*, 1940, *O World*, 1945, *The Life of the Insects*, 1949, after Karel Čapek, and *Errand into the Maze*, 1954.

[Translated from the original German.]

Notes

1. Paul Stefan: *Tanz in dieser Zeit* – Vienna, New York: Universal Edition, p. 95.
2. Friedrich Rosenthal: *Das Kultur-Problem Osterreich*, 1940 Unpublished manuscript at the Austrian Theater Museum, p. 94.
3. Paul Stefan p. 58.
4. *Ibid.* p. 58.
5. *Ibid.* pp. 58–59.
6. Alfred Polgar, Franziska, *Die Weltbühne* Nr. 14 (Berlin 7.4.1925) p. 520.
7. Paul Stefan p. 59.
8. *Die Bühne* 24 September 1925, p. 7.
9. *Die Bühne* 16 September 1926.
10. Paul Stefan p. 59.
11. *Ibid.* p. 59.
12. *Ibid.* p. 59.

Bibliography

Gertrud Bodenwieser: *The New Dance*. Vaucluse 1959
Heinrich Huesman: *Welt Theater Reinhardt*. Munich: Prestel 1983
Barbara Lesak: *Die Kulisse explodiert*. Friedrich Kieslers Theaterexperimente und Architekturprojekte 1923–25. Vienna: Löcker 1988
Shona Dunlop MacTavish: *An Ecstasy of Purpose*. The Life and Art of Gertrud Bodenwieser. Dunedin 1987
Shona Dunlop MacTavish: *Gertrud Bodenwieser. Tänzerin, Choreographin, Pädagogin*. Berlin: Zeichen und Spuren 1992.
Gordon Craig on Movement and Dance, ed. Arnold Rood. London Dance Books 1977.
Rosalia Chladek: *Tänzerin, Choreographin, Pädagogin*. Monograph edited by Gerda Alexander and Hans Groll. Vienna: Osterreichischer Bundesverlag 1965.
Entfesselt. Die russische Bühne 1900–1930. Oswald Georg Bauer (Exhibition catalogue) Munich: Akademie der schönen Künste 1994.
Expressionismus in Österreich. Die Literatur und die Künste ed. Klaus Amann, Armin A. Wallas – Vienna, Cologne, Weimar: Böhlau 1994.

5

THE BODENWIESER STYLE

Edited by Charles Warren

Extracts from Bettina Vernon's archives, lectures, memoirs and notes

Bodenwieser said of Isadora Duncan, "She gave us the first inspiration for an approach to dance which was free of the conventions of previous generations[1]." Her own frequently quoted "Aims of the Modern Dance" which appeared in the program of her 1940 Australian Tour, *The Bodenwieser Viennese Ballet*[2], are:

"Every work of art is the expression, through a form, of an adventure of the soul. It is therefore to be understood that every epoch has its own form of artistic expression, showing so the inner feeling of the soul of the people of that age. We may not ask men of our generation to express themselves in the way of those of past generations; consequently we cannot ask dancers to express themselves in the identical manner as those in the eighteenth century did, the time when classical ballet became the style.

The idea of the new dance is that it has taken up relationship to the great stream of modern life, choosing its topics not only of a fairy tale world of lightness and charm, but of the temporary world in which we are living, a world full of problems and fight, and also of great ideas and developments.

The expressive dance is, like every great art, expressing not only a part of human feeling, but all the human feeling, such as pathos, excitement, joy, as well as desperation, vigor, and exaltation.

The modern dance does not wish to be only amusing and entertaining; it aims also to be stirring, exciting, and thought-provoking. That is the ideal of any real art."

After Bodenwieser's first recital in Vienna during the exhibition staged in 1919 by the Hagenbund New Society for Painting, Graphic and Plastic Arts, Alphons Török wrote[3], "Everything the artist offered was new, uncompromisingly new. For the first time, what for some time had been characteristic of the painting, creative writing and music of the modernist movement was now expressed in dance: the unconditional rejection of tradition and the honest quest for new and purely personal forms of expression."

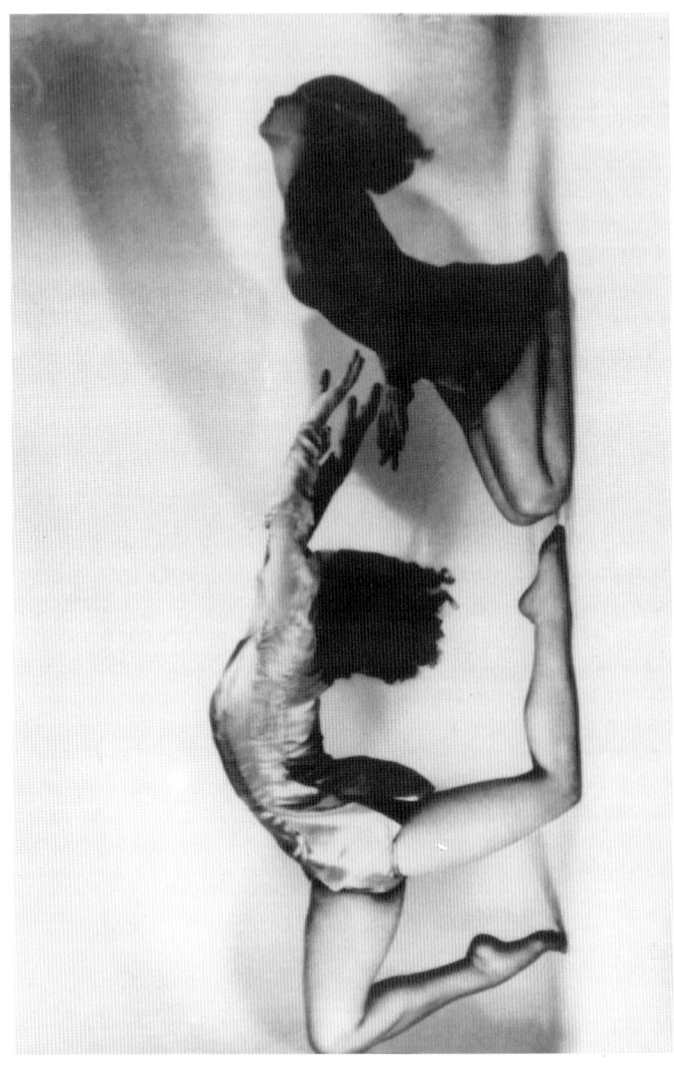

8   Bettina Vernon and Emmy Taussig in "Dance of Farewell" from *Gothic Dance of the Crusades*. A typical backward bend of the Bodenwieser style, 1941.

During the first visit of Bodenwieser's Ballet to Manchester, in 1929, she described her dance *Demon Machine* as showing the rhythm of a machine, which is the essential symbol of our age. "The Machine, like a demon, seizes man and imposes its power over him. He is forced to renounce his personal existence and to become a rotating screw or lever, dominated by the machine, instead of remaining its master." Arnold Haskell wrote of this dance, "These beautiful girls actually became a great, powerful efficient machine and the effect was as awesome and terrifying as the visit to the engine room of some great works, a truly remarkable achievement."[4] He praised the purely dance-based choreography of the theme that was often being expressed in dance at that time and compared it with others he had also seen inspired by the same theme where "flashing lights and real hammers seemed only to defeat the purpose of the invention – Bodenwieser had succeeded where others had not. The dancer should learn to express a subject with his own limbs; the use of accessories showed only a lack of imagination."[5]

The Bodenwieser style is decorative, fluid, effortless, lyrical and dynamic, and displays every kind of human emotion. It embraces movements in circles, spirals, leaps, waves and figures-of-eight with the body flexible and leaning in all directions. Emphasis is placed on flowing arm and delicate hand movements. There is an unimpaired fluidity which commences at the centre of the body and goes in all directions through it to the ends of the limbs. Movements can also be dynamic. In turns, the body can lean in all directions and the knees can be bent slightly. Stress is placed upon each movement of a dance having its corresponding phrase of music and also an appropriate unexaggerated facial expression such as pleasure, charm, fear, determination or remorse.

Jane Turner said of the Bodenwieser live study demonstration she had seen at Sadler's Wells Theatre in 1991:

"What immediately struck me about this Bodenwieser style was its vigorous dynamic, each dancer aimed to project each movement boldly without fear of showing emotion or feeling. I realised how used I had become to seeing blank-faced dancers, coolly *executing* movements. Here was a lively, more vulnerable expression of spirit.

"The exercises we were shown were not, as contemporary dance has increasingly become, aimed at improving technique solely but aimed to increase the individual dancer's expressive range. Exercises that we were shown were colored by interesting impulses: a skipping, fast, travelling exercise developed, we were told, from observing a horse's movements. Other studies were performed to different music, of different tempo, changing the meaning of the steps, using the structures of technique more as a platform from which to express different emotions.

"There is a 'remarkable fluidity, a roundness (which emerges from the center of the body and goes in all directions through the body to the fingertips etc). Movements are mostly continuous and lead into curves. Movement could be fluid or round but also dynamic'.

"She favor[ed] circles, waves, high leaps and turning, with the body leaning in all directions, always using the whole body. [There was] special emphasis on flowing arm and hand movements.

"This bold and direct expressivity was mirrored in body shapes, many reminiscent of the *art nouveau* period during which Bodenwieser was working. To our contemporary eyes these may have seemed rather coy; overtly decorative and pretty perhaps, but attractive nonetheless. This highly visual aesthetic was shown also in the dances we saw on video. The costumes for these dances were elaborate and theatrical. For example in *Sphinx* (1940), the dancer was wearing an exotic and glamorous Egyptian outfit. *Demon Machine* (1924) saw the dancers working on a static point, dressed in futuristic, silver costumes, creating a moving machine through symmetrical, mechanistic movement. *Sunset* (1934) had inspired lyrical use of arms clad in deep red depicting the rays of a setting sun.

"The vocabulary of these dances was not particularly complex, but the movements that the dancers performed grabbed one's attention. There is a direct expressive approach and engagement with theme and emotion rarely seen today in our theaters for dance. As Bettina Vernon suggests, 'Today most types of dance show much brilliance of technique but sometimes the quality of style and expression is lost'."[6]

Of her style Arnold Haskell said, "Bodenwieser is not an extremist and her school is halfway between the classical ballet and Wigman methods. A very nice position which can secure the advantages of both schools."[7]

Bodenwieser said, "For sometimes, timidly and half-heartedly, attempts are made by ballet choreographers to take a few steps into the field of Modern Dance, misusing its ideas by borrowing some of its movements that seem characteristic, having acquired them through short periods of training or by imitation merely as a result of watching Modern Dance performances. To claim, after such excursions that a dancer has 'mastered' the Modern Style does only injury to both. It is still worse when the dancer first belittles the Modern Style then claims to have acquired it without real study 'in addition' to the classical style."[8]

Bodenwieser frequently stated that which is recorded in her book the *The New Dance*:

"No dancer can ever hope to become even a minor figure in Modern Dance without being intelligent, strong in emotions and imagination and with creative ability, without being in short a personality."[9]

This is aptly illustrated by her expressive choreographies of different themes in the notices of programs printed by *The Peterborough Times* [Australia] in the early forties:

"Madame Bodenveeser [sic], who was the first woman Professor of Choreography at the Vienna State Academy, was famous throughout Europe for her modern methods of "streamlined" dancing, and students from many countries have trained by her methods. For more than 10 years there has been a Ballet to demonstrate the "poetry of motion," as evolved at the Vienna State Academy and the dancers have visited the United States, South America and Japan, as well as England and the principal European countries."

* * *

"A delightful program calculated to appeal to every individual taste will be presented."

* * *

"For the "young at heart" there will be such numbers as *Saucy Sailor*; for lovers of sheer beauty there will be such dances as *Christmas Song*, *The Mermaid* and *Eve*; for lovers of sculptured motion there will be *The Sphinx* and *I and Thou*; for those who delight in vigorous numbers there will be *Slavonic Rhapsody*, *Czech Dance*, and *Demon Machine* and for lovers of charm and romance there will be exquisite dances depicting the Vienna of happier days—*The Blue Danube*, *Viennese Waltz* and other lovely numbers."

Notes

1. *The New Dance* by Gertrud Bodenwieser, edited by Marie Cuckson. Private edition. Rondo Studios, Vaucluse, NSW Australia, p. 43.
2. Australian Tour 1940. *The Bodenwieser Ballet Program*. A. J. Tait by arrangement with International Theater Enterprises.
3. Alphons Török, *Wiener Tanzabende: Der Merker*, Vienna 1979. No. 7.
4. Arnold Haskell, *Dancing Times*, October 1929, pp. 13 and 14. "Diaghilev, A Personal Tribute." "Gertrud Bodenwieser, First Impressions."
5. *Ibid*.
6. Jane Turner, *Dice*, August 1991, pp. 10 and 11, "A lost Chapter in Dance History."
7. Arnold Haskell, *Dancing Times*, October 1929, pp. 13 and 14. "Diaghilev, A Personal Tribute." "Gertrud Bodenwieser, First Impressions."
8. *The New Dance* by Gertrud Bodenwieser, edited by Marie Cuckson, p. 93.
9. *Ibid*., p. 90.

6

BODENWIESER TEACHING IN VIENNA AND AUSTRALIA

Compiled by Charles Warren

Extracts from Bettina Vernon's archives, lectures, memoirs, videos and notes, together with Innes Murdoch's verbatim record of grades for a Teachers' Certificate and Examination.

In 1926 Gertrud Bodenwieser was honored by the Vienna State Academy of Music and Dramatic Art, being appointed as the first Professor of Choreography and Stage Deportment there, a position she held until the outbreak of war in 1939. She also held an appointment as Professor at the Max Reinhardt Seminary in Vienna.[1]

She had an inspiring influence on her students and dancers and expected complete concentration, discipline and dedication to their art. Although of stern countenance, she gained the respect of young pupils by treating them as adults in her private school, which she formed in 1926 at the Konzerthaus to prepare them for the State Academy. Bettina Vernon wrote, "Of all the great things that Bodenwieser taught me, the greatest was absolute single-mindedness in my art, which, it is true, has led on occasion to criticism of me being oblivious to all else. Secondly, my career with Bodenwieser and subsequently enabled me to meet interesting people in many parts of the world and visit places which would satisfy my desire for knowledge of Dance, Music and Art. All of which I owe directly or indirectly to Bodenwieser."[2]

The course at the State Academy was for three years in which, in addition to dance, it was necessary to study dance history, costume design, music and anatomy. Unlike Wigman, Chladek and many others in modern dance, Bodenwieser preferred her students to attend classical ballet classes and therefore she had a classical ballet teacher on her staff, but the steps were seldom used in new dances. "Although she put her choreographies free from all traditional forms – in the service of her statements, she wanted the members of her troupe to have training in classical ballet as well as acrobatic and fencing-lessons – as a base for artistic development and to strengthen their bodies and enlarge their horizons."[3]

STAATSAKADEMIE FÜR MUSIK UND DARSTELLENDE KUNST IN WIEN

Fräulein

BETTINA LANZER

geboren in Wien am 22. Februar 1920, hat an der Staatsakademie für Musik und darstellende Kunst in Wien die lehrplanmäßigen Studien in der Schule für Künstlerischen Tanz mit durchwegs vorzüglichem Erfolge vollendet und als Abschluß derselben am 27. Juni 1938 die Reifeprüfung aus dem Hauptfach

Künstlerischer Tanz

mit einstimmig vorzüglichem Erfolge abgelegt. Es wird ihr sohin im Hinblick auf ihre außerordentliche Leistung und Würdigkeit das

AKADEMIEDIPLOM

verliehen.

Wien, am 27. Juni 1938

Der Hauptfachlehrer:

Edeltraud Tauuul

Der kommissarische Leiter der Staatsakademie für Musik und darstellende Kunst:

9   Example of a Diploma from the Academy of Music and the Performing Arts given to Bettina Lanzer (later Vernon), with translation.

THE VIENNA STATE ACADEMY OF
MUSIC AND THE PERFORMING ARTS

Miss

BETTINA LANZER

born in Vienna on February 22nd 1920,

has completed the prescribed course of studies at the

Vienna State Academy of Music and the Performing Arts

in the School of Artistic Dance

with outstanding achievement.

On 27th June 1938 she passed the final examination in

Artistic Dance

for which she was unanimously awarded the highest

distinction. In recognition of her extraordinary

achievement and personal endeavour, she has been

awarded the

ACADEMY DIPLOMA

Vienna, 27th June 1938

Main Subject Tutor   The Head of the State Academy of

Music and the Performing Arts

VERE MATHEWS

presets

The Bodenwieser Ballet

Under the personal direction of Madam Boden-wieser, late of Vienna now of the Vere Mathew's School of Exercise.

Classes now forming for the Dance Drama, Keep Fit Classes, Slimming.

These famous exercises are an ideal form of Physical Culture for women.

MA 2077

Schools Visited
Teachers Courses Arranged

10   Program of Bodenwieser dances presented by Vere Mathews (Sydney) circa 1940/41.

DANCE RECITAL

BODENWIESER

Artistic Direction: Professor Gertrude Bodenwieser
Musical Direction: Marcel Lorber
Graciously assisted by Magda Neeld, with songs.

Piano Solo—I. Praeludium (Bach) .... Marcel Lorber
Sunset (Charles Weigl) .... The Ballet Group
Dance with Golden Discs, Oriental Motive (Arr. by Marcel Lorber)
      Shona Dunlop, Katja Georgiewa, Evelyn Ippen
Mermaid (Chopin) .... Bettina Vernon
I and Thou (Tscherepnin) .... { Evelyn Ippen
                                            { Emmy Taussig
Sphinx (Lorber) .... Katja Georgiewa

THE MASKS OF LUCIFER
Dance Drama by Gertrude Bodenwieser
Music by Marcel Lorber

1st Picture:—Prologue of Lucifer .... Evelyn Ippen
2nd Picture:—Intrigue
      Intrigue: Emmy Taussig; Young Men: Shona Dunlop,
      Katja Georgiewa.
3rd Picture:—Interlude of Lucifer .... Evelyn Ippen
4th Picture:—Terror
      Terror: Shona Dunlop; Woman: Katja Georgiewa; Mai-
      dens: Melitta Melzerr, Bettina Vernon; Young Man:
      Emmy Taussig.
5th Picture:—Interlude of Lucifer .... Evelyn Ippen
6th Picture:—Hate .... Evelyn Ippen and the Ballet Group

Piano Solo—Papillon Concertetude (Lorber) .... Marcel Lorber
Polish Dance (Dvorak) .... The Ballet Group

INTERVAL

Programme continued—

CRADLE SONG OF MOTHER EARTH (LORBER)
Evelyn Ippen, Bettina Vernon, Emmy Taussig

Faun .... Shona Dunlop

Eve (Rimsky-Korsakov) .... Emmy Taussig

The Demon Machine (Mary Mayer) .... The Ballet Group

———

Piano Solo—Paraphrase of Themes, by Johann Strauss · Lorber
Marcel Lorber

Chevslovakia and Peasant Dance .... Evelyn Ippen, Bettina Vernon

———

MAGDA NEELD
Solo—

(a) "Regnava Nel Silenzio" (Donicetti)

(b) "Daughters of Cadiz" (Delibes)

———

TWO NURSERY SONGS

Jack and Jill .... Emmy Taussig, Bettina Vernon

The Saucy Sailor .... Shona Dunlop, Evelyn Ippen

Piano Solo—Rosamunde (Schubert-Fishof) .... Marcel Lorber

The Blue Danube (Johann Strauss) .... The Ballet Group

Vienna Waltz (Johann Strauss) .... The Ballet Group

Ideas and Choreographie of all the Dances by Professor Gertrude Bodenwieser, late of State Academy, Vienna, now of Vere Mathews, School of Exercises, 147a King Street.

Mr. Eric Pearce, by courtesy of Station 2CH, announcing the Groups.

"The Times," 9/1/1937
Vivacious and excellent the Bodenwieser Ballet. Each member of the troupe dances with extreme precision and grace and the smallest of the movements is a pleasure to watch. . . . Finished and exquisite dancing.

"New York Times," 27/8/1936
It is on beauty of the dancers, of audacious flesh of the Ballet-Bodenwieser, that the show can rest its impressive claims, particularly on such combinations of ballet and scenic beauty as is found in the numbers called "Gold Rush" and the "Machine Age."

Arnold L. Haskell (The Famous Critic)
These beautiful girls actually became a great, powerful, efficient machine and the effect was as awe-inspiring and terrifying as a visit to the engine room of some great works. A truly remarkable achievement.

Le Figaro (Paris)
It is the unusual beauty, unsurpassable grace and charm of the dancers that the Ballet Bodenwieser can rest its impressive claims. Such brilliant combination of Ballet and Scenic beauty are truly exquisite.

Den Haag, Dagblad, 29/10/1936
. . . Unusually great, the Bodenwieser Ballet is versatile in its art, quite as graceful as sterling.

Bogota—Colombia (South America)
"El Tempo," 14/8/1938
Again we are amazed at the richness of fancy, the greatness and production.

Tokio—Japan
"Nichi Nichi," 2/4/34
An intoxication of harmony in aspect of noblest movement . . . highest interpretation . . . of ideas . . . of proof of magnificent ability. No spectators left without great admiration, without realisation of having experienced something undoubtedly magnificent

Warsaw—Poland
"Dziennik Wilenski," 7/4/1936
Great artistic ideology. . . . Grand in stature. . . . Unequalled in exportation. The Highlight of the evening, "The Mask of Lucifer." We see the art of mimic of movement in such clearness that they appear to speak, unsurpassable the precision of rhythmic, the beauty of the line of movement, the combination of poses.

Bodenwieser did not give purely technique-orientated classes; students would often be given a theme for a period. A class would always start with basic exercises at the barre, such as plié, combined with loose movements of the head and arms, followed by the wave and figure of eight movements of the feet, legs and arms, and swinging leg movements. "When bending backwards attention was paid to raising of the chest by breathing inwards to show a gradual curving of the back."[4] Some of the movements were developed away from the barre with different interpretations implied by the music. Other movements were circular movements of the arms and body, high leaps and turns. Emphasis was always placed on the flexibility of the body and the importance of flowing movements commencing at the centre and extending to the ends of the limbs and fingertips. Particular attention was paid to delicate hand movements. Practice would be given in making circular movements on the floor look attractive and interesting. Often students had to form a circle around her so that she could more easily see and if necessary correct their movement. Occasionally students were asked to choreograph a short dance or illustrate how they would conduct a lesson to show how well they had absorbed her teaching.

Often sculptural positions would be introduced to show a good expressive line of the body with a smooth progressive movement between them. Bodenwieser had a remarkable talent for noticing and developing latent abilities of dancers and students. She did not hesitate to change the choreography and costumes if it was considered to be beneficial to a dancer and the dance. She was of the opinion that dancers' capabilities could be judged when dancing a waltz. Sir Peter Wright expressed a similar opinion at the Ross Alley seminar *And I Remember*, London, July 1992, when he mentioned that he asked applicants at auditions to dance a waltz.[5]

During her visit to England in the thirties she taught at colleges in Bedford and Birmingham and at the Rutherston Dubsky School. Among those who attended were Frederick Ashton, Antony Tudor and Helen Wingrave. Two schools which taught the Bodenwieser style in London in the thirties were the Rutherston Dubsky and Brooke Elton Schools. She also lectured at the Imperial Society of Teachers of Dancing.

Teaching in Australia

After arrival in Australia, Bodenwieser formed her own dancing school at the Vere Mathews Studios in Sydney and was subsequently asked to give classes at higher education colleges, YWCA schools, and to teachers.

She usually asked members of her Ballet to accompany her as assistants: Evelyn Ippen, Emmy Taussig, Bettina Vernon and Shona Dunlop.

Bodenwieser believed very much in specialist classes. For example, Evelyn Ippen was asked to teach classes of the Bodenwieser leaps; Bettina Vernon, the waltz classes. The idea was to demonstrate the Viennese waltz as a ballroom dance (*Gesellschaftstanz* – social dance) and then develop it later into the Artistic Waltz as the Australians were familiar with the former. Bettina Vernon recalled that they often had difficulty in emulating the Viennese spirit of the waltz but grasped the technical movements remarkably quickly.

At this stage personal relationships between Bodenwieser and her dancers became more intimate compared with those in Vienna. She would now speak in a light and informal way so they became more attached to her. In Vienna she was very possessive and seldom had discussions away from the studio. Bettina Vernon was interested in Professor Wiesenthal's master classes which were being given at the Akademie, and decided to take private lessons with her, in defiance of Bodenwieser's wishes.

Bodenwieser's influence spanned four decades in which her flexibility was shown in the way she could change her teaching methods, choreographies and costumes by giving careful consideration to the ages, abilities and backgrounds of the students and dancers, and the extent to which they could express her wishes.

As well as in Pitt Street, Sydney, Bodenwieser had branch schools at Dover Road and Carlisle Street, Rose Bay, run by Evelyn Ippen and Bettina Vernon, and Shona Dunlop at the Killara Memorial Hall.

Notes

1. *The New Dance* by Gertrud Bodenwieser, edited by Marie Cuckson. Private edition. Rondo Studios, Vaucluse, NSW Australia.
2. Bettina Vernon's private notes.
3. *Tanz 20. Jahrhundert in Wien*, 1979. Translated from catalogue.
4. Bettina Vernon's private notes.
5. Sir Peter Wright, Director of the Birmingham Royal Ballet until 1995.

THE
MODERN SCHOOL
OF EXPRESSIVE
DANCING

Gertrude Bodenwieser

210 PITT STREET.. 1st FLOOR

Branches:

EVELYN IPPEN   BETTINA VERNON

Presbyterian Church Hall, Dover Road and Carlisle Street
Rose Bay — FU 7249

SHONA DUNLOP—Killara Memorial Hall, JX 3727

11   Advertisement for the "Bodenwieser School of Expressive Dancing", 210 Pitt Street, Sydney and two branches taught by members of her Ballet, circa 1940/41.

Bodenwieser's teaching certificate

The following was recorded in 1942 by Innes Murdoch, the first Australian dancer to become a principal dancer in the Bodenwieser Ballet, who recalled that:

"In order to gauge the progress of the Bodenwieser students, it was thought advisable to determine their standard and degree by means of examinations, through which the correct style and system could be faithfully passed on.

Completion of a period of training, therefore, was envisaged to give formal recognition for those who wished to continue – either as teachers or professionals, and to this end Bodenwieser, together with one or two of the English speaking students, formulated the four grades necessary to gain a 'Teacher's Certificate'."

Sections (grades) and teachers' examination schedules

Section 1

1. Leg lifting from hip, with knee bent, toe pointing to ground and leg facing forward – thigh to be raised parallel to ground.
   A. On   (1. Lifting and holding to certain time.
   one   (2. Quick lifting.
   spot.   (3. Lifting, slowly and quickly rising on to ball of the foot.
         (4. Lifting in jumping.
   B. As A, but carried into space.
   C. As A, but moving backwards.

2. Leg lifting to side. (A. Leg rolled in from hip.
                   (B. Leg rolled out from hip.
   Both in 4 ways – i.e. slowly, quickly, on ball of foot, jumping.

3. Quick kicks – to front, and then to side, knee facing upwards.

4. Walking. Slowly, toe to heel.
        "   Quickly, heel to toe.
        "   On balls of feet – quickly.

   Running.   A. Legato.
                  B. As a jump-run.
   Then Running in simple patterns – e.g., Circle, An Eight.

5. Fundamental turning, on own axis with 3 or 4 steps.

6. Standing on one leg – other relaxed.
         Pointing. A. with relaxed leg.
                   B. with stretched leg.
                to front, side, back.
                then diagonal front – diagonal back.

7. As 6, but in kneeling on one leg.

8. BENDING.   (a) *In Standin.* Weight on back foot, other pointed to front. Bending over unweighted foot, head towards knee. *To Side.* One foot pointed to side. Alternate bendings over weighted and unweighted legs – keeping body well facing front.
    (b) *In Kneeling.* – on *both knees.*

Slowly,   (1. Simple bending forward and up
and in   (2.   "   "   to alternate sides.
swinging   (3.   "   "   back and up.
                  On *one knee.* – as (1).

9. Weight changing – one foot pointed to front. And change weight, from front to back leg.
    A. on whole foot.
    B. on balls of feet and down.

10. Arm Movement.   1. SLOWLY lifting arms to side, to shoulder level, and dropping.
     2. Arms lifted from sides – palms up – making small circle so that they drop through centre of body.
     3. Lifting in circle, from centre, out to the side and down, (arms separately, then together) $\smallsmile$
     4. Opening and closing of arms, from centre to side, then side to centre, at shoulder level.

11. Movement combining arms and weight changing. Toe pointed to one side – arms at shoulder height on opposite side. As weight changes from one foot, bring arms in semi-circle to shoulder height on opposite side –
     1. Just slowly.
     2. Then swinging.
     3. Then with side chassé, taking a circle and a half swing with arms – in swinging; in jumping.

12. Combinations of steps – e.g. 2 step forwards; 1 step back; chassé forwards, 2 steps back, any simple combination.

13. Simple amalgamations – not to be longer than 8 or 16 bars.
     e.g. 4 jumps with 4 weight changings,
          2 turns, 4 steps, etc.
     Pupil may choose own amalgamation with the music.

NOTE: For Central European Dancing.

1. When weight is lying on foot or feet, they should NOT be turned out further than the diagonal between front and side.
2. Legs lifted in the air may be turned out from the hip when lifted back and sometimes when lifted to side.

Section 2

All movements as in Section 1, must now be combined with arm movements –
    e.g. jumping with opening and closing of arms.
        running with lifting and dropping of arms, etc.

1. Lifting of leg back, slowly, then quickly.
    A. With leg stretched, and turned out in the hip.
    B. With leg bent 1. hip turned out (attitude)
                        2. hip turned in. (arabesque)

2. Lift left leg forwards, and right leg back, with arms closing over front leg, and opening with leg back.
        1. In walking.   2. In swinging.   3. In jumping.

3. Standing on spot.   1. Right leg swing forwards, swing back and down.
                        2. Swing back, swing forwards, and down.
                        3. Swing across body, out to side and down.

4. Bending back, in standing.
    A. With weight on back foot, other pointed.
    B. With weight on front foot – other relaxed to side.

5. A. Swing right leg forwards, right leg back, then bend forwards, over the left (pointed) leg.
    B. Swing left leg forwards – leg back, step onto it, then bend back, over this weighted leg.
    C. Swing leg across body, out to side, step onto it, and draw other pointed leg up to it, so that body becomes a C.

6. Circling of Body, front side back side, etc.
        A. In standing.
        B. In kneeling – on one knee; on both knees.

7. Weight changing in 4 directions, front, back, one side, other side.
    Work out various combinations, e.g., starting back, starting front, or to one side.

8. Weight changing in kneeling. On one knee, other foot forward.
    Weight forward over front knee – arms open – weight back sitting onto foot, arms closed over stretched leg, and vice versa.

9. TURNS. A. Cross right foot over other, go onto toes, straighten knees, and come down with left foot in front – both feet close together.
    B. Turning with quick little pattering steps, on the same spot.
    C. With leg lifted parallel to ground, but knee bent, and toe pointed, raise in circle from side to cross over other leg in turn as A.

10. Square step. Standing left foot. Right leg step across left. Left leg step back – right leg step to side. Left leg across to starting position.
    Then cut off corners, making it into a circular step, and move into space.

11. Jumps.   A. Double jump – with bent and stretched legs. (Standing on left foot – kick up right leg – and while still in air kick up left leg to it, and land on right leg.)
    B. Fouetté jump.
    C. Short run, kick one leg up, and land with both feet together.
    D. Continuous jumping up and down. Both legs together – kick one leg up.
        1. To front. 2. To side. 3. To back.

12. Step combinations – e.g. a chassé – and lift one leg forwards – chassé – and lift other leg back, etc.

13. Amalgamation of movements – of any movement mentioned – must last for at least 32 bars.

All modern ballroom music excluded from choice.

Section 3

All movements of Section 2 must now be combined with body movement – Body and arms must be taken in parallel and opposition direction to legs.

1. Circling of body – forwards, side, back, side – rising onto toes and taking arms in same circular motion.
    A. In standing.
    B. In kneeling (both knees)
    C. With a short run or chassé, carry the movement from standing to kneeling on one knee, on one circular swing.

2. Simple circling of leg in kick – starting in front, through side to back.

3. Figure movements of arms – in circles, loops, and form of 8, – in any chosen direction.
   1. In standing.
   2. With weight changing – either 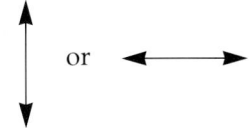 or
   3. With steps.
   4. With jumping.

4. Falling to ground. Straight forward, to side, backwards.
   A. Softly) linking the fall with upright positions
   B. Passionately) – either sitting or standing.

5. Moving forwards or backwards in kneeling and crawlings – with various expressions.

6. Turns – with body bendings and movements.
   A. Quick turning on the spot – simple closing and opening of arms with body bending forwards and backwards.
   B. Quick turning on the spot – with body moving in circles – front side, back side.
   C. Turning with the swing of arms in either circles, loops or 8s.
   D. Reverse, leg taking circular swing from front to back, placing it down at back, and turning with body movement – on spot, then into space.

7. Jumps – A. Fish leap – body curled as a C, backwards, whilst in leap. Arms stretched by ears over head – legs very stretched – all movement comes from waist – legs, hips, backwards from waist; chest, shoulders, head, arms, backwards from waist.
   B. Jack-in-the-Box Jump. Both legs pushed forward into air, and try to touch toes with the hands.
   C. Jeté en tournant.
   D. Chassé. Right leg kick forwards and quickly bend to hit left thigh, then left leg spring out backwards – all in one movement.
   E. Double jump, as a high kick, with body bent backwards on landing.

8. Body Wave. To sides, forward, backwards.
   A. Standing. B. Swinging. C. Jumping

9. Balance Exercises. Difficult walking, with arms and body movement. Various forms of lying, sitting and kneeling, after own choice, and combined with getting up.

10. Pre-arranged by pupil – A. Series of turns and jumps.
    (own choice)   B. Swinging, growing and impulse move-
                        ments.

11. Realisation of Music – into movement.
    A. Walking to certain rhythm.
    B. Walking to patterns in rhythm.
    C. Dynamic of movement soft or strong, slow or quick, light or
       heavy, changing according to the music.

12. Improvisations – expressing either a character, emotion or the music.
    Not longer than 64 bars.

13. TWO Dance solos – (character dances may be included).
    Dances to be choreographed by the Teacher.
    All Modern Ballroom Music excluded from choice.

Section 4

1. Leg lifted from hip with knee bent and toe pointed to ground, combined with wave bend backwards.

2. Bending to side (e.g. left) gradually raising right leg to side, and
   slowly sweeping left arm down line of body into a circle to shoulder
   height, and down.

3. TURNING: A. Taking (e.g. right) leg, and (right) arm, both with a
               circular swing outwards, pelvis well forward and
               turning on the spot.
            B. Same as A, but taking leg and arm with a circular
               swing from side over across front of body.

4. Any free and difficult combinations of body and arm movement, for
   balance – to be done
                    A. On the spot
                    B. Into space.
   e.g. 1. Waves, on one leg, to front, sides, back.
        2. Circles of body – with one leg pointed   A. Front.
                                                    B. Back.

5. A. Develop of leg forward, pelvis well forward, and ending in a
      back bend, taking arms in great circle with the body (taken with a
      chassé).
   B. Develop to side, taking both arms in a circle and in same direc-
      tion as leg, into a side bend, then place leg down, and draw other
      one up to it (also with a side chassé).

6. JUMPS. A. Heel clicking, moving sideways – one leg is held about a foot off ground, whilst other is brought up to click the heel.

     B. A Fouetté jump, with heel click at end before landing.

     C. Grand jeté – a simple high leap after 3 steps, or chassé,
        1. With front leg stretched.
        2. With back leg stretched.
        3. With both legs bent.

     D. Fouetté jump, with a bell clap from the straight leg onto the lifted leg.

     E. Splits in the air. 1. Body facing front, legs to side.
                    2. Body facing front, one leg front, other back.

     F. Double jump in turning.

     G. Jump with front leg stretched forward, other leg bent under it.

7. COMPOSITIONAL FORMS. Turn any given exercise into a compositional form –
e.g. a series of bendings.
      "   "   " turns.
      "   "   " steps and jumps.
Amalgamations of movement in compositional form. e.g. turning and falling to ground; sitting and rising to fully stretched position; turning and leaping.

8. IMPROVISATIONS, to express all the dynamics of music – e.g. crescendo and decrescendo, legato and staccato.
Express the character of music in movement – e.g. sadness, gaiety, struggle, heroism, etc.
Express a character, e.g. an angel, gnome, witch, etc.
Examiners must give 3 well-known characters for choice – of which the pupil may choose ONE for characterization.

9. Solo dances. 2 to be prepared. One may be arranged by teacher.
One MUST be choreographed by the Student.
    All Modern Ballroom Music excluded.

Teachers' Examination.

1. A knowledge of exercises which lead to the harmonic development of the body, which will give it the highest degree of strength, elasticity, suppleness and endurance.

2. A knowledge of exercises, and a knowledge of the VALUE of exercises –
   e.g. What exercises are needed for:
   1. Stretching the spinal column.
   2. Counteracting exaggerated lordosis.
   3. Fortification of muscles of legs and feet.
   4. Fortification of abdominal muscles.
   (These examples only – Pathology excepted).
   All exercise must be given for:
   A. Children
   B. Adolescents
   C. Adults,
   and must be based on a knowledge of physiology and anatomy.

3. Analysis of movement.

4. Knowledge of Physical Education Systems, which have influenced the Dance.

5. Knowledge of the History of the Dance.

6. Knowledge of the theory of music.

7. Knowledge of most popular Folk and National Dances.

Practical

1. A demonstration of exercises, and explanation of method of their teaching to students.
   A. Exercises for Physical Culture.
   B. Exercises for encouragement of a Dance technique.
2. Demonstration lesson, with pupils, lasting not longer than 15 minutes, showing how the physical culture exercises lead into compositional forms.

PART II

CONTRIBUTIONS AND LETTERS FROM FORMER MEMBERS OF THE BODENWIESER BALLET AND MARIE CUCKSON

7

THE EARLY DAYS

Hilde Holger

*One of the members of the original Bodenwieser Dance Group, Hilde Holger
writes in 1960 what she remembers of the early days of Gertrud Bodenwieser
during the 1920s.*

Frau Gerty was what you might call self-made. There was nobody in her
time who could have taught her as much as she demanded. I remember
that in her earliest days she was a pupil of Professor Godlewski from the
Vienna Court State Opera, which was at that time a stronghold of the
classical ballet. She also very diligently went as often as her time would
permit to a first-class classical teacher in Vienna, Irmgard Thomas, who
also became later Frau Gerty's pupil for her own quite new and different
style of work.

Frau Gerty was a most hard-working person. We always wondered how anyone could stand so much work. When she had finished
her classes in the Konzerthaus, or our rehearsals, she went straight away
to the nearby Academy and worked again for hours, and in the evening
when she was free she attended a theater or a party and was still full of
her marvellous energy.

Before she formed the Group, she gave solo performances, and
that was how I came to know about her and to join her classes. All her
dancers first became her pupils, and it was from among her best pupils
that she formed and later recruited her Group. As far as I can remember,
she never took anybody into her Group except her own pupils, trained in
her own, quite new, style.

In these early days (before 1924) she was connected with the
Wiener Hagenbund, a society of modern painters of Vienna which
included Oskar Kokoschka, Wolfgang Born, who painted a portrait of
her, F. A. Harta and others. It was through her connection with these
artists that she came to make her first public appearance, in 1919. She
could at first give only solo recitals, as her approach was too original, but
she gradually educated her audience to appreciate her approach and
attracted dancers such as myself who wanted to work with her.

Of her solo dances I particularly remember *The Chinese Juggler*, a dance of eastern exotic movement combined with her original touch. She stood on a square podium and only moved on a small space, looking very Chinese indeed. Lisa Maria Mayer composed the music, which included a gong, and incense was used to heighten the atmosphere.

Her first classes were held at the Vienna Konzerthaus, and in 1921 she became teacher (later Professor) at the Vienna State Academy of Music and Theatrical Arts. Then all of us who were her pupils went to study under her at the Academy and gained our diplomas there. From that time on she had both her own school at the Konzerthaus and her classes at the Academy.

It was in 1924 that she presented her dancers as the Bodenwieser Dance Group in Vienna. At that time we performed dances composed for the Group with herself sometimes as soloist or in dances with the partner she had at that time, Ernst Walt. One of the early group dances was the famous *Demon Machine*. A beautiful duo dance of Bodenwieser and Ernst Walt was called *Being*: two persons melting into one, to music by Debussy. Both were dressed in grey and the movements were flowing into each other.

The Group consisted of herself and six girls, including myself. About this time, Frau Gerty experimented with us on a round stage, on the occasion of an international theater exhibition. One dance we performed on that occasion was the *Dance Round the Golden Calf*, with an idol (Mammon) in the centre and the dancers circling round to worship it. In the same programme was *Film without Screen*, a rather grotesque idea.

One of the earlier performances of the Group in the Konzerthaus, the biggest stage for dance recitals in Vienna, was in 1928. This included a suite of dances called *Rhythms of the Unconscious Mind*, which was influenced, of course, by Sigmund Freud. The dances which comprised it were *Dream of Flight*, a solo dance performed by Trude Burg, *Dream of Desire*, danced by Marion Rischawy and myself (Hilde Holger), and *Dream of Fear* in which Bodenwieser danced in the centre, surrounded by figures from nightmares.

In the same programme was the *Mystic Dance Vision of the Wonder of the Mango Tree*. Three monks sitting under a tree see a wonderful vision, but a beautiful girl (danced by Marion Rischawy) descends from their dream and the vision disappears.

Also in the same programme was *Decadence*, a satire on the Charleston, with all the stock characters of that time: an old roué, for instance, runs after a pretty young girl. We were all possessed and absorbed in the characters that we had to express and to dance. Marcel Lorber conducted the orchestra.

From that time, Frau Gerty became "The Bodenwieser".

At about the same time, we performed a work called *The Burning Thornbush*, a twenty-minute piece after a drama by Kokoschka.

It was an interesting experiment to dance to music and speech chorus. Kokoschka wanted to express the desire of man and woman, but in a very abstract form. The idea turned out to be very difficult to put into dance form; the time was perhaps not ripe to accept such an experiment, as the public had to be trained to appreciate dance dramas, and this was also a very abstract work.

In these same years (in the 1920s), the theater was also experimenting, and some of the avant-garde producers sought her cooperation as choreographer and engaged her group in their expressionistic productions. She was, at first, the only choreographer who was engaged in this field. Thus she worked under Max Reinhardt, who is recognized to have been one of the greatest men of the theater in our time. Reinhardt produced *The Miracle*, one of his most famous productions, in Vienna in a very large circus, the Circus Renz, and we danced in it. It was unforgettable experience for all of us, and we were very proud to be contributing to it. We did not mind even rehearsing until midnight.

We also took part in Klabund's *The Chalk Circle* and in Karlheinz Martin's production of Wedekind's *Franziska*. Wedekind, a forerunner of such modern writers as Osborne, shocked the public with this play, as it was a drama about a lesbian woman and all kinds of demi-monde characters. We took the part of dancers in the night life of the play, and went with it for a long season to Berlin, where we also gave a recital from our own repertoire.

Bodenwieser was also engaged to make the choreography for her husband Friedrich Rosenthal's production of Goethe's *Faust* at one of the great theaters in Vienna.

By this time the name of Bodenwieser was well-known all over Europe and she was touring regularly with the Group over the Continent and even to England, and later to Japan.

We all loved our work with Frau Gerty, and we were possessed by the dance.

[Based on material held in the Hilverding Foundation, the originals of which are in the possession of Marie Cuckson, 44 Kings Road, Vaucluse, N.S.W. 2030, Australia.]

8

A DANCER SPEAKS

Hede Juer

Hede Juer was one of Gertrud Bodenwieser's first group of dancers. She joined the group in 1922 and remained until 1934. She provides here in 1975 a reminiscence of Bodenwieser's early days as dancer–choreographer and describes her experience of working with Bodenwieser, especially in the creation of Demon Machine, *thus throwing light on Bodenwieser's approach to dance creation.*

The years I spent as a member of Gertrud Bodenwieser's original group of dancers must surely be the most impressive and significant in the lives of all those who had the good fortune to share this extraordinary experience.

She gave us, her dancers, a good deal of freedom to express our interpretation in our own way. While at this time always working with a group, she made use of the individuality of her dancers to complement each other, so as to gain a harmony of expressiveness. There was never a line which made identical movements, as in many other styles of dancing. Not only her rehearsals, but her classes too were an inspiring experience; each class was a new exploration into the possibilities of expressive movement, and no two classes were alike in all those years.

In general, I would say that Bodenwieser's dance choreographies consisted in direct interpretation of the style and mood of the music chosen. For those dances which were intended to illustrate problems of the time, she had a different approach, which I can best explain by an example. Beginning with an idea, she would call together two or three members of her group with whom she had a more personal relationship, to discuss it with them. During these sessions, she would walk up and down, head bent, with her characteristic pose of holding one hand to her mouth, as she searched for the form the idea should take. It was thus that she started to work in 1923 on the idea that developed into the famous *Demon Machine*.

The idea of translating into movement the frightening aspects of mechanization, with the dangerous effects it could have on humanity, excited her imagination to a prophetic fervour. We, the dancers, were immediately fascinated by the idea. It was apparent, however, that the music would have to be equally inspired, and created together with the movement.

To satisfy this necessity, Bodenwieser approached the composer Lise Maria Mayer. Mayer, who was equally taken with the idea, agreed to be present at all rehearsals, to grope with us for sound, rhythm and accents, step by step, bar by bar.

I can say without any exaggeration that for the following weeks we were all under a spell of utmost dedication. We rehearsed three or four times a week for six to seven hours, and Bodenwieser was always the first to arrive and the last to leave the studio in the Konzerthaus. Naturally, as in every artistic effort, there were days of utter depression, days when we had to change what we had done before and to rearrange movements for the sake of continuity or increase of tension, but during that time we were tireless, as people are when they are completely involved in artistic creation. We felt instinctively that we were about to create under Bodenwieser a kinetic masterpiece, the relevance of which concerned the whole world, and which the whole world would understand.

The work fell into two parts. In the first part the dancers moved weightlessly, untroubled by any problems, in paradisal innocence, through space, while Bodenwieser, as the evil spirit of the machine, kept in the background squatting, staring, rigid. Suddenly a crashing chord and Bodenwieser's first abrupt, thumping movement shattered the innocence and peace. Now with ever-increasing force the demon drew the people closer, gradually overpowering their resistance, until they suddenly became grouped in front of the demon as parts of a dehumanised, soulless mechanism, completely under the demonic compulsion. Now the machine began to work, with presses, pistons, wheels, and seemingly all the reciprocating motions that the observer sees who looks into the heart of moving machinery. Gathering speed as it worked, it exerted its unrelenting force and momentum. Music and movement stopped together abruptly, the power switched off. No trace of humanity is left.

That dance was taken round the world, and remained in the company's repertoire for more than thirty years. It always made a great impact on the audiences, who recognised it as an expression of their own problem, a basic problem of our times.

[From a letter held in the Hilverding Foundation.]

9

A NOTE ON "THE FORD SYSTEM"

Hede Juer

An early experiment in expressive movement by Gertrud Bodenwieser.

A new idea of that time (the 20s) which was considered marvellous was the Ford System. Henry Ford had invented the moving-belt method of

12 *Demon Machine* envisaged machines gaining dominance over the human race. Choreographed in 1924.

mass production. This meant that if every worker repeated continuously the same detail-action in the construction of a machine, passing that part on to the next man, who added the next part, and so on, time and money would be saved. Speed and efficiency increased, but it led to boredom and the dehumanisation of every worker.

How to transform that principle into kinetic form? Gertrud Bodenwieser supplemented her group with about ten girls. We were standing side by side, connected by a band in front of each body, each of us doing with her arms her own single movement, which was a continuation of the movement done by the neighbor on her left and a pre-step to the movement of the girl on her right. The rolling of the work bench was simulated by gliding steps to the right in a serpentine design. We started slowly, the gliding and the arm movements increasing in speed proportionally. We gradually lost our human expression and turned into complete robots. The ending, as in *Demon Machine* was abrupt, the power switched off.

[A note held in the Hilverding Foundation.]

10

VIENNA REVISITED IN MEMORY

Helen Elton

On a visit to Vienna in 1927 I was taken to a dance performance of the Bodenwieser Ensemble at the Academy Theater which is adjacent to the Vienna State Academy of Music and Dramatic Art. Two outstanding dance themes were received by the audience with enthusiasm: *Demon Machine* and *The Bells*. The program also included dances which, to me, were the expression of true dancing: flowing, light, at one with the music.

My mind was made up. I seriously wanted to pursue my dormant desire to attempt a career in the art of dancing. Fortunately family circumstances made a longer stay in Vienna possible. After the necessary investigations I was to enrol in Professor Bodenwieser's classes at the Academy, subject to my being accepted.

Meeting Gertrud Bodenwieser was somewhat inhibiting; I was conscious of her ability, or so it seemed, to measure accurately the interest of the applicant. Her appearance was striking: elegant in a simple black dress, medium height, slender figure, fine regular features, straight dark hair with center parting caught in a bun at the nape of the neck, lovely expressive hands. She had an indefinable charm. Passing muster, I was accepted. This was in Autumn 1927.

The excitement of studying under this celebrated creative dancer was indescribable. Bodenwieser's attitude towards her students was inspiring. She seemed to want to draw out whatever degree of talent might be hidden. The method of instruction was to assemble a number of students in a circle; in this way each one could be observed by Bodenwieser when she or an assistant took the class. This also enabled the following group to take note of the corrections and improve their own execution, if possible, of the given movement when their turn came. The warm-up movements were generally in the form of swinging ones: tracing the figure '8', swinging the legs, then arms, circling trunk, head, finally combining all these movements with steps from side to side. *Adagio* exercises followed, slow balancing ones, never neglecting arm and hand movements. Elevation technique was also stressed.

In the choreography classes Bodenwieser often used the square as a basis, enabling varied and interesting space patterns and dance

13 *Aufschwung (Up Beat)*, Helen Elton. A typical Bodenwieser jump, choreographed in 1931. Photo: Yvonne, London.

14 *Cymbal Dance*, Helen Elton and Barbara Brooke. Choreographed in 1931.

sequences. She always encouraged her students to choreograph their own dances. Her attitude was at all times a constructive one, never criticizing in a manner to undermine the confidence of the student. At the end of the summer term there were performances at the Academy Theater. The more advanced students produced their own dances.

At that time I was the only student from England in Bodenwieser's classes and, wanting to share my experiences with friends in London who attended ballet classes with me there, I wrote descriptive accounts, hoping that one or the other would follow up my suggestion to take part in special Bodenwieser courses. This did come about later on.

The curriculum at the Academy included courses in psychology, anatomy and pedagogics. It also involved giving movement classes in the evenings at the recreation centers attended by women in different professions. The directions given were to avoid making the participants feel awkward or clumsy. The movements were specially construed in a manner to make the individual get a feeling of the beauty of movement, never technically difficult or too strenuous. The work-out and the relaxation attained through this form of physical instruction sometimes resulted in the participants applauding spontaneously at the end of the lesson. Very gratifying.

Bodenwieser's sense of music was exceptional. Together with her well known accompanist, the pianist Marcel Lorber, she produced ballets and dance themes of originality and great beauty.

One memorable ballet Bodenwieser produced was for the Festival of Vienna in 1930. As subject she turned to an allegorical theme from the Middle Ages, a legend by Hans Sachs named *Truth*.

Truth appears on Earth in the form of a woman. She hopes to be accepted by the Guild of Craftsmen who are bound by honor and friendship, but is turned away. At a Wedding Feast she is unwanted. At the Court of Law she is again turned away because no one wants to hear the truth. Finally she is accepted by children who represent innocence.

Truth was danced at the première by Edith Richers, one of Bodenwieser's students from Berlin – a gifted dancer with an ethereal beauty. Bodenwieser herself danced the part of the ragged Accused who is attempting to defend his rights in Court. Through her strong portrayal she evoked resounding acclaim. The ballet remained one of the most successful in the repertoire of the Bodenwieser Ensemble.

Trude Burg was another prominent member of the Bodenwieser Ensemble. Her gift for dramatic parts was recognized and she was given full rein in the dances Bodenwieser created, resulting in remarkable success. Trude Burg remained in the Ensemble from 1928 until 1934. Thereafter she took up an acting career. An engagement in Berlin brought her acclaim. At the time she also did dubbing of American films. Subsequently she went to the United States and appeared in several

TEATRO FILODRAMMATICI

**Venerdì 29 Aprile
Sabato 30 Aprile
Domenica 1° Maggio**

GRUPPO DI DANZE

BODENWIESER

LE

6

PIÙ BELLE E BRAVE DANZATRICI DI VIENNA

**PRIMO PREMIO AL CONCORSO
INTERNAZIONALE DI FIRENZE
1931**

15 Notice of the appearance of the Bodenwieser Group at the Teatro Filodrammatici, Milan, in April and May 1931, also stating that the Group had won the first prize at the Florence International Concours 1931.

Programme

Duet from "Don Pasquale" ... ... Donizetti
HELLA TOROS
FERNANDO GUSSO

Two Viennese Songs
HELLA TOROS

Visione Veneziana ... ... Broggi
FERNANDO GUSSO
At the Piano: Dr. M. CARNER

Rondo Brillant B minor ... ... Schubert
ADOLF REBNER
WOLFGANG REBNER

Group of Dances

created and produced by Gertrud Bodenwieser
(of the Vienna Academy of Music)

Costumes designed by Lizzi Pisk, Vienna

1. Cymbal Dance ... ... John Hawkins
   (arranged by Helen Elton)
   Barbara Brooke,
   Helen Elton
   At the Piano:
   The Composer

2. Der Karren ... ... Moussorgsky
   (showing the heavy labour of men whose souls are
   oppressed.)
   Phil Burney, Myra Doniger,
   Jeannette Rutherston
   At the Piano:
   Wolfgang Rebner

3. Entreaty ... ... Bortkiewicz
   Helen Elton

4. Tango ... ... Albeniz
   Phil Burney
   Violin and Piano:
   Adolf and Wolfgang Rebner

5. Farewell ... ... Moussorgsky
   Joanna Sands,
   Helen Wingrave
   Violin and Piano:
   Adolf and Wolfgang Rebner

6. Exuberance ... ... Glazounow
   Jeannette Rutherston
   At the Piano:
   Wolfgang Rebner

7. Cradle Song ... ... Brahms
   Barbara Brooke
   Song:
   Hella Toros

8. Viennese Waltz ... ... Johann Strauss
   Phil Burney, Helen Elton,
   Jeannette Rutherston,
   Joanna Sands, Helen Wingrave
   Violin and Piano:
   Adolf and Wolfgang Rebner

16 Program of a private Bodenwieser dance recital held at the Austrian Embassy, London, 1934.

plays in New York, adding radio broadcasts to her repertoire. Returning to Germany she took up speech therapy and was very much in demand because of her approach through movements based on her original studies of expressionistic dancing with Bodenwieser.

At the beginning of the 30s several dancers and physical training teachers from England joined Bodenwieser's special courses in Vienna. Among them was Jeannette Rutherston, a graduate of the Bedford Physical Training College. She stayed on after the courses and seriously studied Bodenwieser's method of expressionistic dancing. Bodenwieser became interested in her and made it possible for her to take small parts in the ballets when the Ensemble went on tour.

The Bodenwieser Ensemble was much in demand throughout the continent of Europe. One of the leading dancers in the Ensemble was Trudl Dubsky, a petite blonde with a rare gift for lightness of movement and excellent jumping technique, giving the impression of weightlessness. She became interested in Jeannette Rutherston's idea that Bodenwieser's interpretation of the Modern Dance movement should become known in England. Consequently, Trudl Dubsky eventually left the Bodenwieser Ensemble and joined Jeannette Rutherston in London in 1932 to open the Rutherston Dubsky School of Dancing at Great Ormond Street. This school attracted widespread interest and became an immediate success.

Occasionally Jeannette Rutherston and Trudl Dubsky gave performances in which they enjoyed considerable renown. At one such recital at the Queen's Hall in Bradford, the program included three pieces from three Chinese poems by Li-Tai-Fo which, according to a critic, were wonderfully interpreted. The Bodenwieser method was vividly described as, "Specialized rhythmic movement, a type of dancing which is coming very much to the fore by reason of its development of physique, naturally graceful movement and poise." Jeannette Rutherston must have felt gratified that she was able to fulfil her desire to make Bodenwieser known in England.

In 1934 Trudl Dubsky fell ill. Jeannette Rutherston decided to fill the gap of Trudl Dubsky's absence by inviting Bodenwieser to London. Fortunately she was able to accept. The courses she conducted at the school attracted dancers and teachers from the various branches of the profession. It was interesting to observe the reaction of the participants to Bodenwieser's form of instruction which seemed to inspire a general and concerted flow of movement. Her fame was such that she was entreated to return to London.

During Bodenwieser's visit to London in 1934 an Austrian Exhibition was mounted there. It showed the work of renowned painters, sculptors and architects. The then Austrian Ambassador, Baron

Frankenstein, who had the reputation of being an outstanding diplomat, invited Bodenwieser to give a recital at the Embassy. He arranged for a platform to be erected in the ballroom with special lighting. Bodenwieser was delighted to accept and selected a group of dancers.

The program began with *Cymbal Dance* (music by John Hawkins). Dramatic solos had as themes *The Cart* (Mussorgsky) showing the heavy labor of men whose souls are oppressed, *Entreaty* (Bortkiewicz) and *Farewell* (Mussorgsky). The lighter themes included *Cradle Song* (Brahms), *Tango* (Albeniz), *Exuberance* (Glazunov) and to end a Johann Strauss *Viennese Waltz*. It was a successful recital and Bodenwieser seemed well pleased by the appreciation expressed.

Eventually the Rutherston Dubsky School closed because Trudl Dubsky required a longer period of convalescence. Jeannette Rutherston thereupon concentrated her interest in dancing by writing. She became a dance critic and an assistant editor to Philip Richardson of the *Dancing Times*. In that capacity she again enjoyed success.

When Trudl Dubsky finally regained her health, she joined her husband, the celebrated pianist and conductor Herbert Zipper, in the Philippines where he had been invited to conduct the Manila Orchestra. Trudl Dubsky started classes there and in time she was able to form a ballet which was very successful. When war broke out and the Japanese invaded the Philippines Trudl Dubsky and her husband escaped to the mountains and through good fortune were able to flee to the United States.

In New York Trudl Dubsky was invited by the renowned actor manager Erwin Piscator to conduct classes at his workshop there. After three years she left for Chicago where her husband, having gained a considerable reputation as a conductor of the Manila Orchestra, was engaged to teach at the Chicago Conservatory of Music. Trudl Dubsky gave classes there and again had a large following. She eventually accepted an invitation to teach at the University of California in Los Angeles where she remained until she died in 1976.

Among the students attending Bodenwieser's special courses in Vienna and afterwards in London was Barbara Brooke, an excellent all-round dancer. She had been trained in various forms of dancing, including the Margaret Morris Method and also ballroom dancing. Enthusiastic about the Bodenwieser art of dancing, she wanted to open a school and invited me to join her. Naturally I took up her suggestion with alacrity. We duly founded a studio in central London and called it the Brooke Elton School of Dancing. Included in the curriculum was ballet training and tap dancing. Again the Bodenwieser Method attracted a great deal of interest and we were off to a good start.

Grace Cone, the founder of the well known School of Dancing which later was named the Arts Educational School in London, having

JEANNETTE RUTHERSTON   TRUDL DUBSK
Austrian—
Czechoslovakian

THE RUTHERSTON DUBSKY SCHOOL OF RHYTHMIC MOVEMENT
32 GREAT ORMOND ST W. C.I.
Telephone HOLBORN 5331
All Correspondence to
33ᴬ CHEYNE PLACE CHELSEA S.W.3

I hereby certify that MYRA DONIGER, a student at the above school has taken two courses under my tuition, one in June-July 1933, & one in January-February 1934, in the art of Central European Dancing according to my method.

I am completely satisfied by the standard reached by her in her work during these courses.

Gertrud Bodenwieser

State Professor of Dancing
Vienna.

17 A certificate from the Rutherston Dubsky School of Rhythmic Movement signed by Gertrud Bodenwieser in 1934.

heard of the Bodenwieser Method, invited me to give classes. She had Annie Fligg of the Laban School give lessons for a while but she seemed to prefer the Bodenwieser Method. My time there was an inspiration. The students showed keen interest. Grace Cone was one of those remarkable artists and teachers who was always ready to investigate new approaches to the art of dancing.

One day Frederick Ashton, being the great artist he was, and always alert to any new approach to dancing, came to our studio to find out about the form of choreography he had heard that Bodenwieser taught. He was interested in the concept of using the square as a basis for creating spatial variations of dance patterns. After his visit, I must admit, I learned more from his comments about how to draw out choreographic patterns than I was able to convey to him.

Barbara Brooke, who became an outstanding exponent of the Bodenwieser Method, also gave classes in boarding schools for girls and therewith spread it among the young. A few took up dancing seriously afterwards.

In the summer of 1938 I took up an engagement as choreographer and dancer for the Jean Valmy Revue in Paris. One ballet was an interpretation in movement of music by Debussy. The second was a stylized sequence of angular movements in various groupings to music by Olga Kantrovitch, a musician who frequently undertook to compose simultaneously with the choreographer. These ballets were remarkably well received despite their seemingly incongruous insertion in a typical revue program exhibiting lovely, scantily clad girls, witty chanteurs, and sketches.

When war came circumstances changed abruptly and we were obliged to give up the school. In the 50s I joined my husband in Washington D.C. By chance I was invited to give classes at the Recreation Department in the evenings to professional women. These classes became popular and I enjoyed reviving the kind of teaching I had done in my student days working for my diploma. In the local paper, a typical American witty write-up about my classes described them as "The waist wastes away in a waltz."

Through her students Bodenwieser's interpretation of the Modern Dance movement continues to be a strong influence on all branches of dancing.

SALA TEATRU NOWOŚCI we LWOWIE

W ŚRODĘ, DNIA 5. MARCA 1930 R. O GODZ. 7·30 WIECZOREM
NA DOCHÓD SCHRONISKA DLA BEZDOMNYCH

GERTRUDA
BODENWIESER

z zespołem tanecznym

Pp. Gertruda Bodenwieser, — Trude Dobska. — Erna Larkens, —
Miquette Hirmer, — Gisa Pirkan, — Illa Raudnitz, — Marion
Richawy, — Jeanette Rutherstone.

Kierownictwo muzyczne: Kapelmistrz Marcel Lorber

PROGRAM

1. BORTKIEWICZ: Heroiczny marsz
2. CHOPIN: Walc
3. TAŃCE DO NOWOCZESNEJ MUZYKI
   a) POULENZ · Gra linji
   b) MAC DOVELL: Kwiaty
   c) LORBER: »Tchinellentanz«
   PRZYGRYWKA
4. PIEŚNI I TAŃCE LUDOWE
   a) Krakowiak
   b) Staroangielska pieśń ludowa
   c) Pieśń stepowa
   PRZYGRYWKA
5. SYMBOLE CZASU
   a) Mistyka
   b) Maszyna demon
   c) Dekadencja
   OPIESZAŁY ZALOTNIK ALBO CIĘŻKI WYBÓR, — Komedja
   taneczna układu G. Bodenwieser — Muzyka W. A. Mozarta
   Osoby:

Piękna blondynka	Zalotnik
Piękna brunetka	Czarny paź
Służąca	Jasny paź

7. GROTESKI
   a) Parodja tańca wschodniego
   b) Parodja tanga
   PRZYGRYWKA
8. J. STRAUSS: Wiedeński walc

Tańce pomysłu i układu GERTRUDY BODENWIESER
Prof. Akademji Muzycznej w Wiedniu.

Kostjumy Harry Täuber, Arch. Wiedeńskiego Burgteatru.

Nowy fortepian koncertowy Bösendorfera ze składu Kaima i Syna
Lwów, ul. Kopernika 11, — Stroiciel: Karol Fuchs. ul. Łozińskiego 4

18 Details of a Bodenwieser Program during a tour of Poland in 1930.

Konzertbüro der Wiener Konzerthausgesellschaft

GROSSER KONZERTHAUS-SAAL
Donnerstag, den 12. Juni 1930, halb 8 Uhr abends

Anläßlich der Festwochen

TANZGRUPPE
GERTRUD BODENWIESER

Ausführende die Gruppe: Gertrud Bodenwieser, Trude Dubsky, Miquette
Hirmer, Gisa Pyrkan, Illa Raudnitz, Edith Richers, Marion Rischawy
Die Assistentinnen: Helene Byne, Ellinor Geranke
Das vergrößerte Ensemble: Mimi Beck, Loli Petri, Annemarie Juppe
Mitwirkend im 2. Bild: Helen Elton, Hertha Haböck, Magda Hollmann, Irma
Herrmann, Inge Reichelt, Bea Rubelli, Jeanette Rutherstone, Gerda Singer,
Emmi Steininger
Mitwirkend im 4. Bild: Minnie Arenz, Magda Hollmann
Musikalische Leitung: Marcel Lorber   Orgel: Arthur Kleiner
Wiener Madrigalvereinigung — Leitung: Herbert Zipper

WER WILL FRAU WAHRHEIT HERBERGEN?
Tanzspiel nach dem altdeutschen Spiel des Hans Sachs (1494—1576)
Bearbeitung, Inszenierung und Choreographie von Gertrud Bodenwieser
Musik nach altdeutschen Motiven von Marcel Lorber
Kostümentwürfe von Alfred Kunz (D. Volkstheater). Ausgeführt: Atelier Ella Bei

VORSPIEL, das zeiget wie Frau Wahrheit vom Himmel zur Erde geschicket wird, woselbst so viel
Lüge zu Hause ist
I. BILD, das zeiget wie Frau Wahrheit zum Feierabend der Handwerker kommt, woselbst die
Freundschaft zu Hause ist und wie es ihr dabei ergehet
II. BILD, das zeiget wie Frau Wahrheit zur Hochzeitsgesellschaft kommt, woselbst die **Liebe** zu
Hause ist und wie es ihr dabei ergehet
III. BILD, das zeiget wie Frau Wahrheit in ein Gerichtshaus kommt, woselbst die **Gerechtigkeit**
zu Hause ist und wie es ihr dabei ergehet
IV. BILD, das zeiget wie Frau Wahrheit zu den Kindlein kommt, woselbst die kindliche **Unschuld**
zu Hause ist und wie es ihr dabei ergehet

II. Abteilung:
1. HEROISCHER MARSCH . . . .   Marcel Lorber
Zwischenspiel
2. SCHWINGUNGSAUSTAUSCH   Bortkiewicz—Lorber
a) Glocken
b) Sender und Empfänger
c) Ekstatische Kurve
Zwischenspiel
3. WIENER WALZER . . . . Johann Strauß

Kostümentwürfe der II. Abteilung:
1. und 3: Hans Heinz Herbatschek, 2a: Alfred Kunz, 2b und c: Lisl Burger
Idee und Gestaltung samtlicher Tänze: GERTRUD BODENWIESER
Klavier: BÖSENDORFER

Verlag der Wiener Konzerthausgesellschaft, III., Lothringerstraße 20

19   The Bodenwieser Dance Group performance at the Konzerthaus, Vienna,
in June 1930 during the Festival. Bodenwieser had her school there too.

11

WORKING WITH BODENWIESER
IN THE THIRTIES

Emmy Steininger

Emmy Steininger (later Taussig, Towsey) was a leading member of Bodenwieser's company from 1930 to 1943, first in Vienna and afterwards in Sydney, and remained in close contact with her and involvement in her work until the end of Bodenwieser's life and career. She writes about Bodenwieser's approach to dance creation, with special reference to Sunset.

When Gertrud Bodenwieser first took me into her group in 1930, she already had a great reputation not only in Vienna, but throughout Europe. In Vienna, besides conducting her own school at the Konzerthaus, she was Professor of Dance and Theatrical Arts at the Vienna Academy, an experienced choreographer, teacher, and producer. Regular tours took her company to many of the European centers of culture.

The original group had worked with her since the early twenties and she had danced with them, all young women not much younger than herself. With this group she had worked out her revolutionary ideas of dance movement and gained acceptance as an innovator both in content and style. When, as was inevitable, one or other of her dancers left her for new careers or to retire into private life, she selected new members to replace them from among dancers she had trained herself in her own style and spirit.

In those days there was always an enormous choice. Every year between twenty and thirty dancers finished their studies at the Academy, and all hoped to find a place in her group. Those who were not chosen by Bodenwieser usually found a place in one of the many little opera theaters of Europe.

By this time, she already had well-established connections with managers who arranged the tours to the various European centers such as the cities of Italy, Poland and Czechoslovakia. These managers exerted a certain amount of pressure on her to include in her programs dances that coincided with the popular idea of artists from Vienna, especially Viennese waltzes. Although she responded to these wishes with dances of great charm, lightness and humor, it was her experimental dances which absorbed her real interest. It was in these dances that mattered

20 *Sunset.* Bodenwieser was inspired by the national emblem, the sun, when she visited Japan in 1934.

most to Bodenwieser that we of her group gained our most intense experiences. *Sunset* was one of them.

During the tour to Japan in 1934, she came into contact with the lyricism of Japanese art, and it was with the inspiration of this poetic contact that she began to envisage the idea of *Sunset* and tentatively to start preparing it. When we returned to Vienna, she looked for music, which she found in Karl Weigl's *Night Fantasies*, and started seriously to prepare.

Bodenwieser's work on a new dance creation did not begin with the first rehearsal, but long before in the way in which she trained her dancers. The training of all her dancers was based on regular improvisation. The improvisation was the crowning point of every lesson, always eagerly looked forward to. One can only say that it was the magic of her personality which created the mood and conveyed the content of what was to be expressed. Then the dancers, filled with the idea and with a musician equally inspired to improvise, externalised in movement their inner understanding and feeling for the idea. It must be left to be imagined how practised in expressive power those dancers must have been, for whom such an experience occurred almost daily for years. We not only gained a living language of movement, but we exercised it and developed it incessantly, so that Bodenwieser could use us as instruments for the creation of images of beauty, of tenderness or of power. She was the poet who could create such images.

Thus when we started to work with her in *Sunset* we felt we were in the midst of a creation and a part of it. The result was one of her most beautiful symbolic dances, which remained in the repertoire of the company for about twenty years.

I should like very much to be able to explain what it was that made it such an experience for us to work with Bodenwieser in the creation of her most significant and serious dances, such as *Sunset*, but I find it impossible to convey in words. What I can say, however, is that it was never a matter of expressing the obvious surface idea (in the case of *Sunset*, for instance to "imitate" the setting of the sun), but it was a human experience and the direct realization that we were expressing something universal. Indeed it is always so when an idea is given an artistic form by a truly inspired creator: there is something beyond the image itself that is deeper, wiser, and not capable of being explained. The dancers were living in the dance, and the dance was a poetic image for the audience.

[From a letter held in the Hilverding Foundation.]

12

THE EMIGRATION OF GERTRUD BODENWIESER AND HER DANCERS

Emmy Steininger

After a series of strenuous European recital tours in the early thirties, Gertrud Bodenwieser's leading dancers, including myself, received her permission to join, for a time, one of the lavish and financially rewarding revues which were very popular at that time. In 1934 we were engaged under our own name, "The Bodenwieser Group", as a speciality in the Bouwmeester Revue in Holland. During our absence Bodenwieser replaced us from amongst her most talented remaining dancers and continued to produce recitals in Vienna with this second group.

In 1936 the dancers of the first group took another engagement with Clifford Fischer in a revue called *Folies d'Amour* with which we toured to New York and London for a season of some seven or eight months.

When Hitler marched into Vienna in 1938, Bodenwieser organized an exodus for herself, her family, her dance company and Marcel Lorber, her musical director of many years. She contacted her theatrical agents, one of whom, Patek, offered her a tour to South America to perform at the centenary celebrations at Bogotá, Colombia. Another, the famous London agent, Wolheim, wrote that he had sold the *Folies d'Amour* revue, in which the Bodenwieser Group had appeared as a speciality in London and New York, to Williamson and Tait for an Australian season, and that he could sell with it the Bodenwieser speciality to be included in the Australian tour.

Both offers were accepted, and in May 1938 Bodenwieser, with a group of dancers and her musical director, Marcel Lorber, left for South America. There she obtained visas for members of her family, but her husband, Friedrich Rosenthal, who first went to Paris, intending to join her later, was caught by the Gestapo and never heard of again.

After Bodenwieser's departure for South America, I left Vienna for London, where I was joined by the rest of the dancers who were to tour with the revue. We embarked for Australia in January 1939, and the revue opened in Sydney in March, under the title of *The London Casino Revue*.

After the centenary performances in Bogotá, Bodenwieser disbanded her company, so that the various members of it could return to

21   Bodenwieser in *Japanese Sword Dance*, choreographed in 1934.

their families or make their way to the countries of their choice. She had been offered a position in Colombia as professor of dance at a leading educational establishment. She declined, and instead left for New Zealand with the help of Shona Dunlop, a New Zealander who was one of the dancers who had accompanied her to South America. Marcel

Das Echo

Fünf Wiener Tänzerinnen erobern Tokio

Gertrud Bodenwieser ist mit fünf Schülerinnen vor einigen Wochen zu einer großen Japantournee gestartet und befindet sich augenblicklich in Tokio, wo ihr Auftreten und das ihrer Schülerinnen geradezu sensationellen Erfolg hat. Frau Professor Bodenwieser wurde beinahe gezwungen, ihr Tokioter Gastspiel — sie gibt im größten Theater Tokios, im Imperialtheater, Tanzabende — auf zwei Wochen zu verlängern.

50mal Gertrud Bodenwieser in Japan

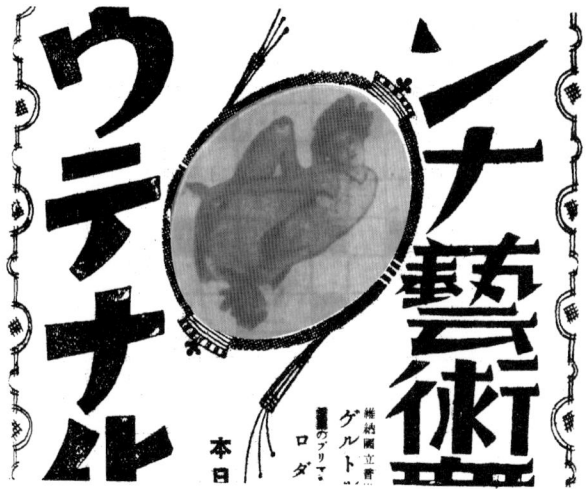

So kündigt eine japanische Zeitung das Bodenwieser-Gastspiel an

Unser Mitarbeiter hatte Gelegenheit mit Dr. Friedrich Rosenthal, dem Burgtheaterregisseur und Gatten Gertrude Bodenwiesers zu sprechen, der folgende Einzelheiten über die Reise und den großen Erfolg der Künstlerin erzählte.

„Meine Frau befindet sich seit 23. März in Tokio. Die Tournee kam durch die Zusammenarbeit eines hiesigen Konzertbüros und eines japanischen Managers zustande. Die bisherigen Tanzabende waren ganz große Erfolge. Meine Frau allerdings schreibt selbst niemals über ihre Erfolge. Sie telegraphierte mir nur: „Gastspiel Tokio auf zwei Wochen verlängert." Aber das sagt mir genug. Außer in Tokio tritt meine Frau und ihr Ensemble noch in ein paar anderen großen japanischen Städten auf. Von Tokio geht die Reise nach Yokohama."

Gertrud Bodenwieser wird von fünf Schülerinnen begleitet, unter ihnen Emmy Steininger und Irma Hermann, die zu den begabtesten Vertreterinnen des Wiener tänzerischen Nachwuchses gehören und von Kapellmeister Marcel Lorbeer.

„Es ist geplant, daß meine Frau im ganzen fünfzig Tanzabende in Japan geben soll", erzählt Dr. Rosenthal und fügt lächelnd hinzu: „Aber — wenn schon ihr Aufenthalt in der ersten Stadt ihres Auftretens verlängert werden mußte, werden es zuletzt wohl mehr sein. Ich habe bis jetzt außer Telegrammen nur einen Brief von meiner Frau erhalten, in dem sie mir ihre Ankunft meldet und erzählt, daß sie im Imperial-Hotel abgestiegen ist, dem modernsten Hotel der Stadt, das ungemein komfortabel ist und unseren Hotels in nichts nachsteht. Außerdem schreibt sie, daß man sich gar nicht vorstellen kann, welche Sympathien ihr als Oesterreicherin in Tokio entgegengebracht werden."

22 *Das Echo* reports on the sensational success of Bodenwieser's 1934 tour of Japan and the two week extension of the tour which increased the number of performances to fifty. Vienna 1934.

Lorber and a few of the company who did not wish to return to Vienna went with her.

She stayed only a few months in New Zealand. By this time our engagement with *The London Casino Revue* had come to an end, and she decided to join us in Sydney forthwith. With this, the emigration was completed, and enough dancers were with her again to form the nucleus of a new company.

Bodenwieser's twenty years as a famed dancer, choreographer, producer and teacher in Europe had ended. Her company was scattered, her family separated from her, her possessions lost, but she had managed to get together with a few of her dancers and her musical director at the other side of the world. She opened a studio in Sydney and soon again began to give recitals. Another period of twenty years began, during which she toured regularly all over the Australian continent and to New Zealand, India and South Africa, and so became again a pioneer of the modern dance, this time for the Southern Hemisphere.

[From a letter held in the Hilverding Foundation.]

13

"I ALWAYS REMAINED A BODENWIESER DANCER"

Evelyn Ippen

I grew up in a little village in Czechoslovakia and was taken by my grandparents to a performance of *Swan Lake* at the Prague Opera. I was so impressed that I danced all the way home. I danced to the music from an old gramophone and had to perform for all our visitors, who thought I was very talented.

When I moved to Vienna, where my parents lived, my mother took me to ballet classes, first to a teacher whose name I cannot remember now, and then to Rudi Franzl who lived close to my home. Today I can say that I was very disappointed and found his classes very boring and uninteresting.

It was then decided that I should join the children's class of Gertrud Bodenwieser, who specialized in Modern techniques, and I will try, although it is difficult after so many years, to describe it.

Madame Bodenwieser was a very strange woman, not as pretty as my mother. She reminded me of a picture of a Spanish woman I had seen somewhere: black hair drawn tightly from her forehead, black trousers, and pearls. She studied me for a long time through glasses which were later described to me as 'lorgnettes'. She seemed very strange, not fairylike, unsmiling, and a bit frightening.

I started in the children's class with Frau Elli, her assistant, a pretty woman. I loved to go to her classes and decided again that I wanted to be a dancer. In the classes we had to skip with slightly bowed knees and pointed toes and the arms did not have to be bowed like bananas, as in classical ballet, but could be used like the wings of birds or butterflies. The frightening gnomes we had to dance had to be done with heavy stamping, quick running steps and jumps although the arms could be used as we liked. Finally there were improvisations which we did ourselves.

On one occasion Frau Gerty took a class herself and it was then that I changed my mind about her. I saw suddenly that she was quite different from other people I had seen, more original. Her movements were more delicate, not easy to copy, and she spoke to us as adults which made us feel more important and enthusiastic. This was my second impression of her.

Two years later my mother decided that I should take the examination for dance at the Academy of Music and Dramatic Arts. My mother was a great balletomane, and would have liked me to go to Professor Dubois who also taught, but I insisted I continue to train with Frau Gerty.

I joined the classes at the Academy and loved them. The freedom of movement appealed to me in the fantasy world in which I often lived. I loved to dance so much that I would dance all the way home: I would jump, turn, my arms flowing in all directions, so that my father would insist that I walk home properly. I continued to go to classical classes, but found them boring, and would deliberately do things that were wrong.

I changed my mind very much about classical dance in later years. Today I find it fascinating: the clearness of line and steps that flow together; the long graceful arm movements; the steps and turns that so surprisingly fit into such a strict form. I still have the feeling, however, that something is missing, but cannot put it into words. I am sorry that I did not study harder as a child as classical dance can be of great advantage in the study of Bodenwieser's. It can make it more understandable, which seldom happens in modern dance nowadays. The full use of expression of the whole body, the beautiful flowing lines, the great energy that is put into the strong movements, all of this can give something extra to the world of dance today.

Of Frau Gerty, I have only superficial knowledge, as she was a very private person. What I do know of her is only in her professional capacity. I remember her as very active and she never seemed tired. I never saw her take a rest. She often stood in a corner and tried out movements or sat at the piano with her Musical Director, Marcel Lorber, who played a major part in her career. He was a great pianist who composed beautiful music for her ideas. (I think she never forgave Bettina and me for taking him away from her when we left the ballet for our tour of Japan and the Far East and some of the performances we did before that.) She was very intelligent, not only interested in dance but also in music, art, literature and in current affairs, which she often symbolized in her dances, as in the dance she called *Terror*. She changed my life: I was always a little frivolous, but with her encouragement I became interested in the world of art and became dedicated to the art of dancing. I was still never close to her, although I became the principal dancer in her ballet company. I also became one of her assistants, and was often praised as one who could show her style and technique in the way she envisaged it; she, herself, was never a great technician. I never had a long conversation with her about things outside the profession, and I often wondered if other members of the ballet were any closer to understanding her strange personality.

I cannot say much about her style of dance; in her words "a dancer should be seen and not described". She was a wonderful teacher and was most astonishing in the style and variety of movement that she could create from a simple idea. For example, from a circle she could create many lessons, combinations of legs and arms, twists and leaps, expressing both the commonplace and using the idea as a springboard to the more bizarre and absurd. Most of her lessons were based on this concept.

She also created many interesting leaps; one of them is now known as the 'Spiral Jump'. It was not easy, and many technically proficient dancers had difficulty in managing it. In her school I conducted the elevation class which was very interesting.

I joined the Academy and before I graduated I became a member of the 'Ensemble', as Frau Gerty used to call us. There were six members, sometimes seven, all with different personalities. Some were strong in expressing movements, some very graceful and lyrical, but all of us had to be versatile. We had many opportunities to travel. We went to Poland, Rumania, Czechoslovakia, Italy and Japan. We also gave a recital in the Konzerthaus and an open air performance in the Burggarten after I graduated from the Academy. The group also went to Moscow to give performances there (although I cannot remember the name of the theater, which I doubt is still standing). From there, we travelled on the Trans-Siberian Express to Vladivostok and then by boat to Japan.

The train ran both day and night, and we only stopped for two hours in towns in Siberia. They were small towns, and I remember seeing many people bundled up in shaggy, dirty furs. Men with fur hats and women in colorful, large headscarves all came to see the train. There were many children begging for sweets. I think the trip on the Trans-Siberian Express was perhaps the most moving experience I had of all the travelling during my career. There we were, two to a compartment and quite comfortable, in contrast to the Russians who travelled in crowded, cramped conditions. It was hard to believe the difference. The train was well heated, which was fortunate as it was bitterly cold outside. I could write much more about this trip: the white snowy landscape that changed every day, the sunsets over Siberia that turned the snow pink and then lilac; it was all very beautiful. We heard wolves howling at night, far away in the distance.

We practised our dancing in the corridor and we also had English lessons with Frau Gerty. I can still see her in my mind when the train stopped in one of the towns, striding along the platform in black pyjamas, with white lace tied around her head, along with our musical director Marcel Lorber in red fur slippers, an overcoat, and a red woollen scarf tied like a turban around his head. All the Russians on the station pointed and giggled; it must have looked very strange to them.

23   Bodenwieser's welcome in Japan, 1934.

We arrived in Vladivostok and it seemed a horrible town, dirty, poor and smelly. Japan, in contrast, was very nice. We danced in Seoul, Korea, and then in Tokyo. It was a very interesting city, even in 1934. We performed in all the big cities: Kobe, Osaka, Yokahama and many others. I will never forget how beautiful it seemed in spring with all the cherry blossom against the dark trees, the Japanese girls in colorful kimonos dancing around them. This ritual dance was called the *Sakura-undo*, and I was to dance it often in the years to come. I visited Japan again in 1947 when I was sent, with my partner, by the Australian government to entertain the occupying forces. Standing in the ruins of Hiroshima, I remembered how it used to be. Tokyo, however, was still a beautiful city. The glitter and the colorful lights were still there. I remembered Frau Gerty, in 1934, saying as she stood by the Japanese flag in front of the Imperial Hotel, "What an interesting flag you have". To which her companion replied, "This is the land of the Rising Sun". It was at that moment that Frau Gerty was inspired to create one of her most beautiful dances, *Sunset*. Perhaps she knew that we were soon to reach the end of an era; two years later war broke out and the peace was no more. Bettina Vernon and I reconstructed the dance *Sunset* for the International Festival of Dance '90, Vienna, which we taught to dancers of the Vienna State Opera Ballet. We revived five of her dances; two solos were for Marialuise Jaska, a principal dancer. One of the dances was *Demon Machine* created by Frau Gerty long before she became famous. *Demon Machine* is a simple dance for five dancers (sometimes seven) and still fascinates the audiences who see it. It is astonishing that such simple choreography, originally conceived for five girls, can still create such an effect after so many years and is still fresh and not dated.

Another dance drama choreographed a few years before war started was *The Masks of Lucifer* which consists of three dances and two interludes. I was cast in the role of Lucifer. The most dominating of the three dances was "Terror" in which Lucifer walks stiffly in a square around people begging for mercy. The women, children, and warriors, all being terrified, fall dead at his feet. The third drama was created to illustrate the words:

'Race against race
Class against class
Mass against mass
Victory is Hate'.

This is very similar to a ballet choreographed by Frau Gerty in Vienna, called *The Pilgrimage of Truth*, in the mid 1930s. It takes its inspiration from an uninviting world where nobody but the 'Innocence of the Unborn' will give shelter to the Truth. In creating this work, I think Frau Gerty was almost clairvoyant.

I spent several years in her Ballet Company, during which she created some wonderful dances. My favorites include *Dance with golden discs*, which although not technically demanding by today's standards produced some wonderful patterns and combinations, and *Olympic Games*, to a Strauss march. This ballet used two girls: Miquette Hirmer, a tall, beautiful blonde, and myself. We were dressed in silver and silver helmets. Another favorite was *Steppenlied*, a kind of folkdance, with brilliant red costumes. Gertrud Bodenwieser was also a master of the Viennese waltz.

In 1938 it was all to come to an end. Frau Gerty left her home town of Vienna and went with a group of her dancers to Colombia. I went to Australia with her first group, and she joined us there with Marcel Lorber. We had an engagement with Williamson and Tait, and then when Frau Gerty came we were engaged at the Minerva Theater.

Starting another school was not easy, but it was a success and she had many pupils, some very talented. I became her Assistant. She developed a syllabus, or method of teaching, for which Emmy Towsey and I became Examiners. Her most talented pupils were Innes Murdoch, Coralie Hinkley, Bettine Browne and Eileen Cramer. Bettina Vernon and I were also teaching in a ballet school for Estelle Anderson. We had many talented pupils too, and a successful children's school. It was then that we began to do our own choreography.

24   *The Sphinx ...* comes to life. Danced by Evelyn Ippen. Choreographed 1940.

The Bodenwieser ballet made many tours of Australia, and fame came very quickly. She started to include more solo dances in her performances, including one called *The Sphinx*. It was created for another of her dancers, but I believe it was I who made the dance a success. It took its inspiration from an Egyptian mural, and showed a stone which became human with all a human's emotions, but within the constraints of the stylised form of the mural. (This dance was also included in the dances we revived at the Vienna State Opera). The second solo in the programme was *The Mermaid*, danced by Bettina Vernon. Frau Gerty also created a ballet *Cain and Abel*. I portrayed Abel and Shona Dunlop Cain.

It was not long before Bettina Vernon and I decided to form our own group. Although we danced under other names and occasionally had a guest artist, we became known mainly as *Ballet for Two*. We choreographed our own dances and included some of Bodenwieser's in our programs. At first Bodenwieser did not forgive us for having left her company, but we were reconciled after our successes in Australia which helped her to become well known throughout the continent.

In 1947 we were asked by the Australian government to go to Japan to perform for the Occupying Forces. We were very well received and decided to go to England afterwards, where we were immediately employed by the Arts Council for a countrywide tour. We danced in small towns and small theaters as well as in London at the Embassy Theater, the Royal Festival Hall, the Fortune Theater and the Usher Hall in Edinburgh.

In 1947 we returned to dance at the "Erstes Fest des Tanzes" in Vienna with Harald Kreutzberg and other well known dancers. Here, too, we included some of Frau Gerty's dances in our program and brought her name back to her home town. This pleased her very much and she finally forgave us completely for leaving her.

In 1960 I was stricken by a very serious illness which I managed to survive, but the light of dancing went out of my life. For a long time I was very unhappy although I managed to keep in training and in shape. Then, in 1989, we were asked to revive five Bodenwieser dances for the International Festival of Dance '90, Vienna and for the Vienna State Opera Ballet. It was a rebirth for me despite the fact that it was too late for me to perform myself, the only thing I would like to do again in my life. It was a wonderful success, but Frau Gerty did not live to see her last great triumph, as she died in 1959, not very old, but active to the end. It would have made her very happy to see her dances performed in the Vienna State Opera House.

Although, after I left Frau Gerty, I trained under many teachers, including Sigurd Leeder whom I greatly admired, and at the Northcote School for Classical Ballet, London, little changed in my established style of dance. I remained what Madame had made me, a real Bodenwieser dancer.

14

BODENWIESER'S LASTING INFLUENCE FROM 1926 TO 1995

Bettina Vernon

Taken by Charles Warren from Bettina Vernon's notes and drafts prepared prior to her death.

For many, particularly those in the artistic professions, early experiences could have a lasting influence upon their lives, as can a teacher. This was the case for me with Gertrud Bodenwieser.

My great-grandfather decided that he would like to own a theater. He started one which he named the "Danzer[1] Orpheum", near Wasagasse 33, Vienna. Here Kurt Jooss and Sigurd Leeder gave recitals accompanied by Marcel Lorber, Gertrud Bodenwieser's musical director and composer who eventually joined our group *Ballet for Two*. My grandmother and mother were very interested in the Vienna Secession, and in a small way were associated with the Wiener Werkstätte and the Werkbund. I have tapestries and their original designs by Professor Otto Friedrich, who was a founder member of the Vienna Secession with Gustav Klimt, a friend who had a studio in the garden of our family villa where the roses inspired some of his paintings. As a family, we were always interested in the arts, and entertained many of its exponents at the villa in Purkersdorf and various flats in Vienna. Alfred Grünfeld the pianist and Edmund Eysler the light-opera composer are but two. It was wonderful for me as a child to improvise dances to their music which I overheard.

One day, when in the garden with Professor Friedrich, I said to him, "Look at this flower; how sad. It looks as if it is dying". He asked me to show him how a flower grows and wilts. Perhaps it was because of my childish efforts of expression that, when I told my mother I wanted to learn to dance, he suggested I should be taken to see Gertrud Bodenwieser. He felt her style was more expressive than the classical ballet of that era, after he had seen it at Duncan's and Wiesenthal's recitals and, somewhat later, Bodenwieser's.

The idea of meeting such a great dancing teacher was rather scaring. I had the wildest dreams. What will she ask me to do? What will she look like? I imagined a very pretty lady dressed in a delicately colored flowing dress interviewing me in elegant surroundings; however my dream picture did not measure up to reality. We went down a dark staircase to a very unadorned studio, the Holländersaal. The 'pretty lady' was somewhat frightening. She was a lady in black, with ebony black hair tied back, of stern countenance, dressed in a black jacket and flared trousers, sitting on a high stool by her pianist, Marcel Lorber, whose musical talent was to be closely connected with my dance career for the next four decades. Bodenwieser asked me first to improvise leaves dancing in the wind and two of my own ideas: I chose the wilting rose and Andersen's *Little Match Girl*, a favorite story, often read to me by my mother. I was accepted, and thus my association with Bodenwieser began, first in the children's class, then in higher classes after private lessons, and later at the "Staatsakademie für Musik und darstellende Kunst" in Vienna.

A time of great excitement each year was the performance of students of Bodenwieser at the Akademie Theater, a leading theater which had a most suitable stage for dance performances and wonderful lighting. Both of these have been of equal importance to me throughout my career, as is also a good pianist, so vital for creating the right atmosphere. These performances were shared with Professor Gross's students; Gross himself had previously been a student of Bodenwieser. Frau Gerty was always very determined not to be influenced by personal wishes of the students: I remember being almost heartbroken when I hoped to dance a Chopin waltz, and she instead chose a solo dance *Fast zu Keck* (*Almost too cheeky!*) to music by Reger. Probably she was correct in her choice in view of the review.[2]

The possessiveness of Bodenwieser towards her pupils could be a problem. In my case she expected me to be restricted to one teacher only for "Artistic Dance". Grete Wiesenthal was appointed professor at the Academy in 1934 and ran a masterclass. Being very fascinated by her technique and personality, I announced one day to Frau Gerty that I would like to study under Wiesenthal as well. She replied: "I do not think it is necessary to attend her classes as well as mine;" however, I took the big step and went privately to Wiesenthal's flat at Modena Park, where she taught her favourite pupils in her salon. After her classes she would often ask us to tea; we had lively discussions about dance and also private matters. I found her classes very fascinating as well, and I was very proud to have two such famous teachers, totally different in their teaching and character.

One day Frau Gerty said she wanted to have a talk with me, which made me wonder what I had done wrong as she very seldom discussed personal affairs with us. She wanted to know if I would like to go with her second company to Holland and dance in it. She was choreographing special dances for the Bouwmeester Revue, the Radetzky March

25 *The Mermaid* (*Die Nixe*) choreographed for and danced by Bettina Vernon. The last dance choreographed in Vienna before Bodenwieser had to leave in 1938.

and other dances. The solo dancer was a senior member of her ballet, Gisa Pyrkan, and I was also to be given solo parts.

I then returned to the Academy to complete my training for the diploma where Frau Gerty choreographed for me her last dance before leaving Austria, *The Mermaid.*[3] When starting to choreograph *The Mermaid* she said to me, as she would say to other dancers, "Here are the music and the story; try to improvise it". She would then take a few movements which she liked and include them in her choreography.

Travelling to the Academy for an evening class shortly after the *Anschluss*, I remember noticing the sunset, red like a flame, dramatic, unnatural and ominous. On arrival I found everyone in tears. Frau Gerty was not there; she had been forced to leave. She had left for Paris with her husband who was subsequently killed by the Nazis. Her letter of resignation said:

"Herewith I declare that I resign my post at the Academy and that I relinquish all rights to further salary with the effect from the day of my departure abroad, 29.3.1938. Signed Prof. Gertrud Bodenwieser."

I stayed to complete my training under Grete Wiesenthal at the Academy and obtained my diploma: Akademie Diplom für Künstlerischen Tanz, mit vorzüglichem Erfolg und ausserordentlicher Leistung (Academy Diploma in Artistic Dance with the highest distinction).[4]

After Frau Gerty left Vienna I danced for Wiesenthal in the opera *Die Willis* (Puccini) at the Akademie Theater and she also taught me one of her dances. I took part in a film with Hans Rühmann *The Thirteen Chairs* and then I went on a tour to Switzerland and Holland with Wiesenthal's Viennese Ballet Group. I was very lucky to hear from Frau Gerty, who was then in Paris. She asked if I would like to go with the Bodenwieser Ballet to Australia. I absolutely loved the idea. It was proposed that we should dance in the Casino Revue *Around the Clock* in Melbourne and Sydney; the engagement was with the biggest theater company, Williamson and Tait. In the revue we danced *Demon Machine*. It was one of the most acclaimed dances and in 1932 had won a bronze award at the Concours International de la Danse in Paris.

One day I was astonished but very pleased to receive the following letter from Frau Gerty, who was now on tour with her second company in Bogotá, but nevertheless very sad at its contents.

Colón
Teatro Colón
Bogotá
1 August

My Dearest Herzerl![5]

I was absolutely delighted to hear from you. Yes, for me too it was a terrible disappointment that nothing came of the English plan. However, the recent news from my husband in Paris implies that sooner or later the Australian tour may possibly come off. But mind you, my husband does write that the people themselves do not exactly know what they want and what is about to happen. But whatever happens, it is my most ardent wish to have you with us again, and I do hope that sooner or later this will definitely happen. Is there any chance of you being able to come to South America? I don't mean necessarily up to the altitude of Bogotá, but if we were to travel on to one of the other states? Could you pay a part of the journey yourself, were you to get an engagement financially favorable enough to include travel costs? Of course I still do not know what will become of us. Are we going to find contacts? And if so, will it be possible for all the girls to stay? *If one or the other might wish to return home, whilst we continue, I am thinking of calling out a good dancer such as you, my sweetie, at my expense.* But as the travel costs are so very high I would like to share them, as otherwise I would hardly manage them. The journey out to here, which is most complicated and requires a three hour flight at an altitude of 3000 m, will cost 200 D.

We have great successes and the whole time on the boat I worked like mad with the girls, and now they have really become a group. I am *delighted* with your successes, my dear, and I did not expect it to be any other way. I often think of the Chopin Etude – the last memory of your dancing which I have carried with me all the time. The pain of parting brings tears to my eyes whilst I am writing this. My dearest child, how I would love to see you again. Since we parted I have been experiencing difficult times but I don't wish to write about them. My husband, sister and nephew are all in Paris and we have many personal worries. Enough of that, and I want to tell you about our work. Every day we dance in the Teatro Colón, a most beautiful theater. We perform *Sunset, Demon Machine*, four solo dances, Chopin: *In Flight, In the Round, Cain after Fratricide, Maria's Vision, Viennese Waltz, Slavonic Dance* and the whole Mozart Ballet, but on points.[6] Hilary and Hilda as the Beauties and Poldi as Amor. Do please write to me by air mail and answer my queries.

Do please greet your dear parents; thank goodness that your brother is well again. Where did Dr. Waltuch go? Also all your dear relatives?

I send you all my affectionate wishes and you, my child, are embraced with fondest love by

Your teacher

[Translated from the original German.]

Bodenwieser in Bogotá[7]

Bodenwieser, although baptized a Roman Catholic, was considered Jewish according to the Nuremberg laws, and was also disliked by the Nazis because of her liberal concept of Classical Ballet and her daring choreographies. She left in 1938 with part of her group (15 dancers, among them Magda Brunner-Lehenstein, the daughter of the Austrian Consul in Colombia), for Colombia, where she had been invited by the Mayor of Bogotá to participate in the celebration of the 400 years since the foundation of Bogotá (*Viennese Revue*). The visa for a 12 week stay was extended and then followed – together with other emigrants Hugo Wiener, Cissy Kraner, and Eugene Strehn – tours through Colombia. The diverse culture of the 'indigenous' inspired Bodenwieser to new choreographies into which she integrated Amerindian music and dance movements. Before 30,000 spectators, this group together with Indian and black dancers performed in the Bullring of Bogotá. In 1939, Bodenwieser followed the dancer Shona Dunlop to New Zealand where she toured several months. She then worked until 1940 in Melbourne (Australia) before becoming domiciled in Sydney.

AUSTRALIAN TOUR, 1940

❖

The
VIENNESE
BALLET

❖

Direction: A. J. Tait
Presented by: Concert Management
Pty. Ltd.

SOUVENIR PROGRAMME

26 Program of The Viennese Ballet touring Australia in 1939–40.

AIMS OF THE MODERN DANCE.

"Every work of art is the expression, through a form, of an adventure of the soul," says Madame Bodenwieser. "It is therefore to be understood that every epoch has its own form of artistic expression, showing so the inner feeling of the soul of the people of that age. We may not ask the men of our generation to express themselves in the way of those of past generations; consequently we cannot ask dancers to express themselves in the identical manner as those in the eighteenth century did, the time when the classic ballet became the style.

The idea of the new dance is that it has taken up relationship to the great stream of modern life, choosing its topics not only of a fancy fairy world of lightness and charm, but of the temporary world in which we are living, a world full of problems and fight, and, also of great ideas and developments.

The expressive dance is, like every great art, expressing not only a part of human feeling, but all the human feeling, such as pathos, excitement, joy, as well as desperation, vigour, and exaltation.

The modern dance does not wish to be only amusing and entertaining; it aims also to be stirring, exciting, and thought provoking. That is the ideal of any real art."

MADAME GERTRUDE BODENWIESER

MARCEL LORBER

Marcel Lorber is a graduate of the Vienna State Academy of Music, where he studied under such famous professors as Leschetizki and Gruenfeld. The latter in his early years was a great friend of Johann Strauss, Jnr., and it was through Gruenfeld that Marcel Lorber became an ardent devotee of Strauss.

Mr. Lorber, who has been identified with Madame Bodenwieser's work for a period extending over 14 years, has composed music for many of the dance-dramas created by Madame Bodenwieser.

In addition to acting as musical director for the dancers, Mr. Lorber is also the solo pianist at all of the Bodenwieser Ballet's dance recitals.

Programme

NOTE:—A section of the theatre will be illuminated at the conclusion of each dance thus enabling the audience to read the programme annotation prior to the performance of the next number.

PART I.

PRELUDE—Grande Minuet (Schubert) · Marcel Lorber

1. MEMORIES OF VIENNA (Johann Strauss) Melitta Melser, Emmy Taussig, Bettina Vernon, Evelyn Ippen

   The Waltz is considered the most perfect expression of early Vienna—city of Beethoven, Schubert, and Johann Strauss. But the gaiety and the joy of life in Vienna are mingled always with a little sadness.

2. FAREWELL (Moussorgsky) Emmy Taussig, Bettina Vernon

   Depicting the tragedy of two human beings who are forced to part.

3. DANCE OF THE ARABIAN BOYS (Glazounoff) · ·
   Evelyn Ippen, Hanny Kolm

   This dance typifies the characteristics of the Arabian boys—alternately playing and quarrelling.

EMMY TAUSSIG

EVELYN IPPEN

PROGRAMME continued

4. THE INCONSTANT PRINCE   -   -   -   Ballet Group

(Inspired by a fairy tale of the Eighteenth Century and set to music of Mozart.)

CHARACTERS OF THE PLAY.

Cupid - - - - - - -	Bettina Vernon
The Fair-Haired Lady - - -	Emmy Taussig
The Dark-Haired Lady - - -	Bettine Browne
The Servant Maid - - - -	Shona Dunlop
The Prince - - - - - -	Evelyn Ippen
The Fair-Haired Page - - -	Melitta Melser
The Dark-Haired Page - - -	Hanny Kolm

Two young Princesses sit preening themselves—assisted by a serving maid—in anticipation of the arrival of the Prince, who is to choose one of them for his bride. They become envious of one another, and a quarrel ensues. The Prince appears, heralded by his two Pages. Cupid brings the Prince a golden apple, which is to be presented to his chosen lady. The Prince, however, is delighted with the charms of both Princesses, and is unable to

Continued on next page

BETTINA VERNON

BETTINE BROWNE

PROGRAMME continued

THE INCONSTANT PRINCE---continued

make a choice. He sinks on the floor in bewildered fashion, and falls asleep. The two Princesses are annoyed at the Prince's indecision, and in contemptuous fashion take up their position again on their chairs. Cupid re-appears and in mischievous mood causes the two Pages and the two Princesses to be mutually attracted, and the two Princesses then disappear on the arms of their gallants. The Prince, on awakening from his dreams, is surprised to find that the Princesses have vanished. In alarm, he implores Cupid to bring them back, but the little god of love is thoroughly enjoying the situation, and he accordingly brings the ugly serving maid in place of the Princesses. The vacillating suitor is overcome with mortification, and his state of mind does not improve when the Princesses re-appear with their sweethearts. Too late the Prince learns that both of the beautiful girls are lost to him forever.

5. BARBARIC DANCE   (Percussion Instruments)   **Hanny Kolm**

Hypnotised by the power of his sword, the savage dances his Bar-baric War Dance.

6. HUNGARIAN FOLK DANCE Evelyn Ippen, Emmy Taussig

Continued on next page

SHONA DUNLOP   *HANNY KOLM*

PROGRAMME continued

7. PIANO SOLO—"Rhapsodie in G Minor" (Brahms) - -
Marcel Lorber

8. EVE (Rimsky-Korsakoff) - - - - **Emmy Taussig**
Depicting the evolution of Eve, who, while still innocent, is tempted
for the first time, and finally succumbs.

9. SLAVONIC DANCE (Dvorak) - - - **Ballet Group**

Some of the vigorous and passionate feelings of the Slavonic people
are vividly expressed in this musical and colourful dance.

INTERVAL

PART II.

I. WATER LILIES (Macdowell) **Evelyn Ippen, Emmy Taussig**
The water lilies wave softly in a tropic water. The waves that have
brought them together for a period may soon separate them again
—perhaps forever.

Continued on next page

MELITTA MELSER

PROGRAMME continued - PART II.

2. DANCE OF THE MEDIAEVAL HANDICRAFTS
(18th Century Motifs, arranged by Marcel Lorber.) **Bettine Browne**
In the 15th and 16th centuries, craftsmen had their various dances representing the handicrafts such as tailoring, carpentering, boot-making, etc.

3. SARABANDE - - - **Evelyn Ippen, Bettina Vernon**
Sarabande Dance originated from the Spanish Suite. Its character is essentially ceremonial, and the influence of the Spanish Court strongly noticeable throughout.

4. CART DRAWN BY MAN (Moussorgsky) - **Evelyn Ippen, Hanny Kolm, Shona Dunlop**
This dance depicts the straining, the pulling and the dragging of man, and his exhaustion and revolt against his fate.

5. VIENNESE MAIDEN (Ziehrer) - - - **Bettina Vernon**
Representing the joyful spirit of a young Viennese girl, displaying, also, a little sadness which inevitably lies close to the heart.

6. THE DEMON MACHINE (Mayer) - **Ballet Group**
This dance is characteristic of the vital problems of this era, demonstrating how the machine is gaining ascendancy over the souls of the people, whereas the people should dominate the machine.

7. DANCE OF THE CYMBALS (Lorber) - **Evelyn Ippen**

8. THE SNAKE CHARMER (Scott) - - **Shona Dunlop**
In India there exists a sect of weird people who, whilst in a trance, have the mysterious power of hypnotising the snake. During the trance the "charmer" frequently develops sudden fits of passion, working into a state of auto-intoxication.

9. CZECHOSLOVAKIAN PEASANT DANCE (Weinberger) **Evelyn Ippen, Bettina Vernon**
This dance is based on the folk lore of the Czech race, reflecting the rustic humour of the people.

10. PIANO SOLI - - - - - - **Marcel Lorber**
(a) La Cathedrale Engloutie - - - - - (Debussy)
(b) Voices of Spring - - - - - (Strauss-Gruenfeld)

11. BLUE DANUBE (Strauss) - - - - **Ballet Group**
"Do you recall that night in June upon the Danube River?"

GOD SAVE THE KING

The VIENNESE BALLET

– in –

Dance Creations by

MADAME GERTRUDE BODENWIESER

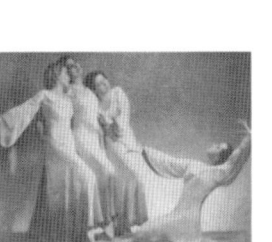

To Australia with the Bodenwieser Ballet

In 1939, dancers of the Bodenwieser Ballet left Europe on the *Maloja* for a tour of Australia which Frau Gerty had arranged with Williamson and Tait.

Needless to say we practised every day and gave performances on the long voyage. On arrival in Melbourne we went immediately to the theater for rehearsals with the producer of the London Casino Revue to arrange where our dances would fit into the program. *Demon Machine* and a Viennese waltz were the greatest success. Dancing the former every day was extremely demanding, especially for those taking the parts on the floor; it was hard on our knees and legs! The Melbourne press took great interest in the Bodenwieser Viennese Dancers who became the talk of the town! The Revue was also performed in Sydney and Adelaide. The dancers were Evelyn Ippen, Emmy Taussig, Bettina Vernon, Katja Georgieva, Melitta Melser and also Katrin Rosselle who became a well-known actress and left for America, and Anna Roth who returned to England.

Bodenwieser's pioneering in Australia

The start of the Bodenwieser pioneering work in Australia commenced in 1939 when she rejoined her first group after leaving Colombia. It included tours of the Ballet, lectures and teaching young Australians in her school. At this stage she was joined by a New Zealand dancer, Shona Dunlop, who had been with her in Colombia. In a very short time Frau Gerty compiled a programme for dance recitals to be given in her newly adopted country. Some of her most famous compositions were restudied: *Demon Machine, Cradle Song of Mother Earth, Farewell, Dance with golden hoops, Dance with golden discs, Sunset* and the dance drama *The Masks of Lucifer*, which in my opinion was Bodenwieser's greatest creation, and in which Evelyn Ippen danced the leading part. It is important to remember that Bodenwieser would often change the choreography to a small extent when new dancers took over parts, to make the most of individual dancers' particular talents. In this her freedom of style can again be seen.

As we were called the Bodenwieser Viennese Ballet, the Australian audience expected Viennese waltzes as well as music by Austrian composers. Naturally one of the group waltzes she created in Australia was the *Blue Danube*, later *Caprice Viennois* to Fritz Kreisler's violin solo. In earlier days Kreisler had been a personal friend of Frau Gerty. This was a dance with four dancers in beautiful waltz dresses,

27 *Voices of Spring*. Choreographed in the Bodenwieser style by Bettina Vernon and Evelyn Ippen, 1944.

28 Bettina Vernon in *Epilogo*, choreographed by Bodenwieser in 1943.

designed by Evelyn Ippen. In it I portrayed a violinist; I also took the Viennese waltz solo *Voices of Spring*. Two ballets in lighter vein were *The Inconstant Prince*, choreographed in Vienna, and *Cinderella of old Vienna*, choreographed in Australia, 1940, the title role being created for me. As the Australian audience had to be educated to the Free Dance, these dances were a way of enabling them to become familiar with the *New Dance* more easily than the more complex dance dramas.

In Australia Frau Gerty enjoyed greatly meeting people from other arts and having controversial conversations with them at the Meriola. It might well have been called "The Meeting House of Various

Arts", a building standing in park-like grounds. Painters, designers, dancers and sculptors all had apartments there. It was a great place for discussion, and out of their talks dances were born. One of the artists was the sculptor, Arthur Fleischmann, who showed many of his works at a Sydney exhibition, "Art for the Ballet and Dance" in 1944. He also cooperated with Bodenwieser for a ballet: *Gothic Dances of the Crusades* consisting of four dances: "Dance of Farewell", "Dance of Gallant Fight", "Dance of Prayer" and "Dance of Happy Return". Frau Gerty and Fleischmann asked Evelyn Ippen to dance the Warrior and me to dance the Warrior's Wife. These dances were popular, especially as they were performed during the war years.

On with the tours

These were mostly arranged by A. J. Tait with the International Theater Enterprises and often demanded very long train journeys to reach our destinations, such as Perth. These journeys provided ample time for discussions in which Evelyn and I often said it would be marvellous to bring the Bodenwieser style back to Europe. Frau Gerty had vowed never to return to Vienna, and I had always hoped that one day we might be able to form a small company and dance there again. Little did we think that our dream would eventually come true.

The Bettina Vernon and Evelyn Ippen partnership: continuation of the Bodenwieser Style

Eventually we decided to form our own small company which later became known as *Ballet for Two*, although we occasionally danced under other names to meet the wishes of agents; we also had a male guest dancer from time to time.[8]

When leading dancers leave any Ballet in order to form their own group, it is a matter of regret and so it was in our case. Frau Gerty was very upset for some time to come, perhaps more so in her case because of her possessive character. After some time she began to appreciate that we owed success to her wonderful training over the years and the experience she had given us; in that way our achievements were not seen to be in competition, but rather as a complement to her style and teaching, particularly as we did not depart from either.

We started rehearsing and soon we had choreographed most of the program which included some of our favourite Gertrud Bodenwieser dances: Evelyn as *The Sphinx* and *Swinging Bell*, and myself as *The Mermaid*,

"CONTINENTAL"

In the Garden of, and in aid of, the
CARPENTER MOTHERCRAFT HOME

25 SHIRLEY ROAD, WOLLSTONECRAFT
SATURDAY, 8th MARCH, 1941, at 8 p.m.

★

EMMY TAUSSIG
EVELYN IPPEN
BETTINA VERNON
MELITTA MELSER
BETTINE BROWNE
SHONA DUNLOP
STELLA ZAHARA

★

Musical Direction:
MARCEL LORBER

Dances originated by
GERTRUDE BODENWIESER

Assisted by
LEONI FEIGL, RENEE BRONNECK
and SIGMUND SPERLING

The Bodenwieser Ballet has danced before the King and Queen of England, and the Queen of Holland. It is a complete unit, and has appeared with brilliant success in London, Paris, and Vienna, in New York and in South America.

Madame Bodenwieser, who was the first woman Professor of Choreography at the Vienna State Academy, was famous throughout Europe for her modern methods of "stream-lined" dancing, and students from many countries have trained by her methods.

Three Viennese girls, two Czecho-Slovakians and one Australian and one New Zealander are included in the group of dancers, and the musical director, Marcel Lorber, is a gifted Viennese pianist.

The Committee:
Miss Carmichael (Matron of the Carpenter Mothercraft Home), Mrs. Graham Shirley, Mrs. J. T. Lloyd, and Miss Catherine Grant (Hon. Organiser of the "Continental").

29 *Czechoslovakian Polka,* choreographed and danced by Bettina Vernon and Evelyn Ippen in 1940. This was the first dancer choreographed by members of the Ballet to be regularly presented in Bodenwieser programs in Australia.

30 Bettina Vernon and Evelyn Ippen at an open-air rehearsal of their Bodenwieser program on tour in Japan, Spring 1947.

Voices of Spring and *Parody of Classical Ballet*. When still in the Bodenwieser Ballet we had choreographed a *Czechoslovakian Polka* by Weinberger and *Death and the Maiden* to Schubert's music. It was the first time in Australia that Bodenwieser had given permission for dancers to perform their own choreographies.

When our dreams began to become reality we did not become rivals of Bodenwieser. But many times there was great competition, as we frequently toured for CEMA (The Australian Council for the Encouragement of Music and the Arts) and had the same agent as Frau Gerty's Ballet. We also appeared at the same venues, but of course not on the same date.

As Bodenwieser had made choreographies for operas at the Konservatorium, we were asked to choreograph some dances for *The Bartered Bride* which we much enjoyed doing. We were also asked to teach the Bodenwieser style to different organisations. At the National Fitness Council, lessons were given to teachers who were taught simple dances which they, in turn, could teach to students.

The first full-length ballet we choreographed was *L'Aiglon*, the story of Napoleon's son, The Duke of Reichstadt. As we needed an arrangement of the music, we asked the director of the Conservatoire in Sydney if he would send us somebody who could arrange a Mozart sonata. A young man came and was most enthusiastic; it was (now Sir) Charles Mackerras. Evelyn and I also started a school for children in Rose Bay, Sydney, where we had another young student from the Conservatoire, Patricia Tuckwell, later the Countess of Harewood. Students of ours who subsequently joined Bodenwieser's all-Australian Ballet were Carol Huxtable and Elizabeth Russell.

We were often asked to perform for charity. Lady Wakehurst, wife of the Governor of New South Wales, and Lady Gowrie, whose husband was the Governor-General of Australia, came to our recitals and always very kindly extended their patronage to us.

When the war had finished, travelling was difficult; however, Marcel Lorber, who by then had joined us, had the idea of going to Japan. The Australian Forces Director saw our Company and engaged us for six weeks to entertain the troops in Japan. At first we were worried that our dancing might not be acceptable to the troops; however, we were delighted when our tour was extended to six months and enabled us to return to Europe on a troopship.

While in Japan we danced in bombed-out Hiroshima. One hall in which we gave a charity performance for Catholic children did not have a roof. As it was daylight, birds could be seen flying across the stage while I was dancing *Voices of Spring*. The Mayor of Hiroshima showed us the building, still partly standing, where the atom bomb fell. It was a

31 Japanese press interview in 1947 with Marcel Lorber, music director, composer and pianist for the Bodenwieser Ballet, in which he refers to his passion for netsuke.

dreadful experience to see Hiroshima and look down on streets where thousands of melted bicycles lay. The Mayor explained that the wind had changed and turned the fire into an inferno.

The return of the Bodenwieser style and choreographies to Europe, 1947

After Japan, Evelyn and I were set to realise our ambition of bringing the Bodenwieser style ballet back to Europe and Vienna. We arrived in England and were fortunate to be introduced to different personalities: Sir Steuart Wilson, the Director of the Arts Council, and Arnold Haskell, who came to see a demonstration of our dances and recommended to Sir Steuart that it would be a very good idea to show this style of dancing in Great Britain. Although in her early days Bodenwieser had appeared several times in England, her style was not really known. We toured for

Walzer in Hiroshima

Zwei Wiener Mädl tanzen über Kontinente

„Wenn Sie über mich schreiben", bat mich Bettina Vernon, die gegenwärtig einige Tage in Wien weilt, „dürfen Sie auch meine Partnerin Evelyn Ippen nicht vergessen. Wir sind seit zehn Jahren beisammen und machen zu' sammen das „Ballet for two" aus. Und der dritte im Bunde ist unser Klavierbegleiter, der Pianist Marcel Lorber. Was also wollen Sie über uns wissen?"

Erzählen Sie doch, wie Sie zusammengekommen sind!

„Evelyn und ich kannten einander schon von Wien her. Wir waren beide Schülerinnen an der Akademie in der Tanzklasse von Frau Professor Bodenwieser. Ich habe außerdem eine Zeitlang bei Grete Wiesenthal und auch im Ausland klassisches Ballett studiert. 1939 stellte Frau Professor Bodenwieser eine Tournee nach Australien zusammen. Vier Monate vor Kriegsausbruch fuhr eine Gruppe von uns auf acht Monate Engagement hinüber. Und als der Krieg kam, blieben wir natürlich drüben. Bald darauf machten Evelyn und ich uns selb' ständig und gründeten das „Ballet for two", „Ballett zu zweit", würde man hier sagen, zu dem dann später Marcel Lorber stieß.

Wien in Asien

Wir kennen den australischen Kontinent viel besser als die meisten Australier, denn wir haben im Laufe der Jahre drei Tourneen durch das ganze Land gemacht. Die Australier haben sehr viel Sinn für Tanz und sind auch selbst sehr begabt. Besonders unsere wienerische Note löste den größten Beifall aus."

Und nach dem Krieg?

„Nach dem Krieg begann die Zeit unserer großen Tourneen durch Asien und Europa. In Asien tanzten wir in verschiedenen Städten für

Bettina Vernon tanzt Dvorak unter japanischer Kirschblüte

die britischen Streitkräfte. Soll ich Ihnen zuerst von Japan erzählen?"

Im atomgebombten Hiroshima

Wir waren im Winter und im Frühjahr in Japan, sahen den Fudschijama im Schnee und tanzten in Tokio und allen größeren Städten, darunter auch in Hiroshima."

Wie sieht es dort aus?

„Die Stadt ist vollkommen zerstört. Keine Stadt Europas ist so völlig vernichtet, wie Hiroshima. Das Feuer hat in den Straßen ent-

Evelyn Ippen im „Tanz der Freude" auf dem Strand bei Sidney

setzlich gehaust. Noch als ich dort war, sah ich auf dem Boden tausende halb geschmolzene Fahrräder liegen. Die Besitzer waren verkohlt oder erstickt, aber die Räder lagen noch herum. Nichtsdestoweniger wimmelt es in Hiroshima von Menschen. Es wird intensiv aufgebaut und darum macht diese Stadt des Todes heute fast einen lebendigeren Eindruck als die anderen japanischen Städte. Wir tanzten dort für Kinder. Natürlich fanden wir in der zerstörten Stadt keinen geeigneten Saal. Schließlich tanzten wir in einer zerbombten Halle ohne Dach und Fenster bei natürlichem Licht. Als Marcel Lorber als Solo den Frühlingsstimmenwalzer in der Bearbeitung von Grünfeld spielte, flogen die Vögel herein und schauten, was hier los war."

...und wieder Reisen!

„Wurde es ein Erfolg? Haben die Japaner denn überhaupt Verständnis für unsere Tanzformen?"

„Gewiß! Sie interessieren sich für europäische Musik und für europäischen Tanz. Harald Kreuzberg war vor dem Krieg in Japan und wir haben bei unserem Aufenthalt noch Leute getroffen, die von ihm schwärmten."

„Wo waren Sie nach Japan?"

„In Hongkong zum Beispiel und in Singapur. Dann kamen wir nach Europa und traten in London, Amsterdam, Paris, Wien (beim Musikfest) und vielen anderen Städten auf. In der nächsten Zeit werden wir in England und Irland auftreten."   h. s.

32   Bettina Vernon's Viennese newspaper interview (1948) describing her career and her tours with Evelyn Ippen, and mentioning their charity performance for children in a bombed out, roofless building in Hiroshima.

the Arts Council for a few years to upwards of 150 venues in England, Wales, Ireland, Scotland and as far as Stornoway.

Performances in the cities were organised by the Anglo-Austrian Music Society, by Otto Harpner and Walter Foster[9] and also by Concert Artists Promotions. We appeared in Manchester and the Usher Hall, Edinburgh, which was rather frightening: two dancers on a large stage with one piano in a completely full house. It worked out well, however. We gave recitals in London in the Fortune Theater, the Embassy Theater, the Park Lane Theater and also danced at the Royal Festival Hall. At Australia House Sir Thomas White, the High Commissioner, and Lady White attended our recital with Lord and Lady Harewood. We appeared in *Picture Page* on British television in 1947.

Now back to Vienna. We danced at the Konzerthaus where Bodenwieser had had her private school before leaving Austria. It was the "Erstes Fest des Tanzes", 27 June 1948, after the war and the program consisted of the following: Harald Kreutzberg, the Grete Wiesenthal Ballet, Lillian Moore, Hilde Baumann, *Ballet for Two*. So, the Bodenwieser style came back to Vienna. The press gave us very good notices and we appeared on the News Films. In *Blind Date*, a novel by Berta Ruck, published in 1953, two chapters feature *Ballet for Two*: "That couple of gifted young dancers who, with their pianist, took the entire evening's performance on their shoulders, were a sensation in Vienna." (Berta Ruck died in 1979, a week after celebrating her 100th birthday.)

We then toured Holland and Italy, returned to England, and composed quite a few new choreographies. One of my favourite dances, which Evelyn and I had choreographed in Australia, was called *Resignation* (an elderly Viennese dancing teacher in a flashback to earlier success in her youth).

In 1992 Walter Foster wrote on the occasion of the fiftieth anniversary of the Anglo-Austrian Music Society:

"Vienna's singular gift to the world of dance is the waltz. Ballet has never really taken root the way it did in London, nor did it ever enjoy comparable popularity. Yet there were some notable Austrian contributions to the art, especially those linked with the names of Gertrud Bodenwieser and Grete Wiesenthal.

In *Ballet for Two* we brought an exhilarating dance programme, mainly of waltz rhythms, to many a remote place – this in the 1950s, long before Sadler's Wells ventured far into the provinces. Evelyn Ippen and Bettina Vernon, two able and attractive ballerinas of the Bodenwieser school, were partnered by that inimitable and infinitely accomplished Viennese pianist Marcel Lorber. This modestly proportioned show, costumed and produced by Otto Diamant, played to full houses and earned much praise and applause. In later years, excerpts were included in our production of *Die Fledermaus* at the Royal Festival Hall and elsewhere."[10]

II. INTERNATIONALES MUSIKFEST
DER WIENER KONZERTHAUSGESELLSCHAFT

SONNTAG, DEN 27. JUNI 1948 / 20 UHR

GROSSER KONZERTHAUSSAAL

ERSTES

FEST

DES

TANZES

HARALD KREUTZBERG

LILLIAN MOORE

HILDE BAUMANN

EVELYN IPPEN – BETTINA VERNON

BALLETT GRETE WIESENTHAL

Klavier: Bösendorfer / Programmpreis 60 Groschen

33 Program for the First Festival of Dance, Vienna, 27 June 1948, when the Bodenwieser style returned to Vienna with Evelyn Ippen and Bettina Vernon.

PROGRAMM

| I. TEIL |

BALLETT GRETE WIESENTHAL

Eine kleine Nachtmusik (1. Satz) . . . . W.A.Mozart

Die Jünglinge   Eva Bernhofer
                 Erika Knicza
Die Kokette   Lia Werner
Die Lustige   Gelli Wolf
Die Sentimentale   Vilma Kostka

HILDE BAUMANN

Thema mit Variationen . . . . W.A.Mozart
Danse funèbre . . . . J. Sibelius

BALLETT GRETE WIESENTHAL

Die Fahne (Revolutionsetüde) . . . . F. Chopin
Lia Werner, Erika Knicza, Vilma Kostka

HILDE BAUMANN

Danza . . . . H. Collet
Launen . . . . A. Dvořak

BALLETT GRETE WIESENTHAL

Weinlesefest . . . . J. Strauß
Am Flügel: Marta Wiesenthal

Kleine Pause

| II. TEIL |

EVELYN IPPEN — BETTINA VERNON (Ballet for two)

Bande der Harmonie . . . . J. Brahms
Das Gewissen . . . . M. Lorber

Ein Mensch, der sein eigenes Gewissen im Spiegel zu erblicken vermeint, versucht diesem zu entrinnen. Jedoch sein Gewissen folgt ihm überall hin nach. Der Mensch versucht zu entfliehen, stürzt sich auch in unmäßigen Rausch und sucht endlich sogar Erlösung in der Welt des Jazz. Im Glauben sich befreit zu haben, versucht er erneut in den Spiegel zu blicken, wo er aber aufs Neue seinem Gewissen begegnet. Er weiß nun, daß es kein Entrinnen gibt.

LILLIAN MOORE

„Skizzen vom Leben hinter der Bühne"

1. Lampenfieber . . . . Leo Delibes

Die Szene spielt hinter dem Vorhang in der Oper unmittelbar vor dem Debut einer jungen Ballerina. Diese Idee fand ihren Ursprung in Gemälden von Degas und wurde von Agnes de Mille für den Tanz bearbeitet.

2. Amazone — 1880 . . . . F. v. Suppé

Eine kleine Elevin des Balletts erlebt eine endlos mühselige und eintönige
Probe. (Miß Moore's Kostüm ist eine authentische Reproduktion eines Probe-
kostüms aus dieser Epoche.)

EVELYN IPPEN

Sphinx . . . . M. Lorber

BETTINA VERNON

Glückstrunken . . . . M. Lorber

LILLIAN MOORE

Tritsch-Tratsch-Polka . . . . J. Strauß

EVELYN IPPEN — BETTINA VERNON (Ballet for two)

Wetterhäuschen (Ein seltsamer Traum) . . . . M. Lorber

Am Flügel: Christiane Hévin de Navarre und Marcel Lorber

P a u s e

| III. TEIL |

HARALD KREUTZBERG (Tänze und Gestalten)

Tanz des Zeremonienmeisters . . . . Scott

Teufelsbeschwörung . . . . F. Wilckens

Sternenlied . . . . F. Wilckens

Drei irre Gestalten . . . .   *   *   *

Aus einem alten Kalender . . . . W. A. Mozart

(Frühling, Sommer, Herbst und Winter)

Am Flügel: Friedrich Wilckens

Im Rahmen der diesjährigen

SOMMER-AKADEMIE DES MOZARTEUMS

gibt

HARALD KREUTZBERG

begleitet von Herrn Friedrich Wilckens einen Tanzkurs in der Zeit vom 15. bis 31. Juli.
Der Kurs findet wie im Vorjahr in dem idyllisch gelegenen Mattsee bei Salzburg statt.
Die Teilnehmer sind im Studentenheim des Mozarteums untergebracht.
Anmeldungen und Anfragen sind zu richten an das Sekretariat der Internationalen
Sommer-Akademie, Salzburg, Mozarteum, Schwarzstraße 26.

USHER   HALL

First and Only Appearance in EDINBURGH

Saturday, 2nd December, 1950, at 7.30 p.m.

Under the Auspices of The Anglo-Austrian Music Society

Concert Artists Promotion Company announces

VIENNESE DANCERS

in their unique presentation of

BALLET in VIENNA

EXPONENTS OF VIENNESE GRACE AND CHARM

EVELYN IPPEN . BETTINA VERNON

POPULAR   VIENNESE   MUSIC

MARCEL   LORBER

After   successful   Australian   Tour

MAGNIFICENT COLOURFUL COSTUMES

DAZZLING LIGHTING EFFECTS

Programme Excerpts :
JOHANN STRAUSS: Tales from the Vienna Woods, Blue Danube, Augustin ;
WEINBERGER : Bohemian Polka ; BRAHMS: Bonds of Harmony ; CHOPIN : Mermaid ;
LORBER : Conscience, The Weatherhouse, Sphinx, The Witch ;
RICHARD STRAUSS : Rosenkavalier Waltz

Tickets : 8/6, 7/6, 6/6, 5/6, 4/6, 3/6, 2/6

**From Methven Simpson Ltd., 83 Princes Street, Edinburgh (Central 5414)
and at door**

34   Leaflet advertising the Viennese Dancers' performance at the Usher Hall, Edinburgh, 1950.

35 *Porcelain Pas de Deux*, specially photographed by Houston Rogers for *The Sketch*, 21 May 1952. By permission of the Theatre Museum, London.

After giving up performing, my partner, Evelyn Ippen, and I were privileged to pass on Bodenwieser's artistic legacy and Austria's contributions to the development of the Free Expressive Dance. Professor June Layson invited us to reconstruct Bodenwieser dances for MA students at the University of Surrey. We were also engaged by Doctor Gerhard Brunner, Director of the Vienna State Opera Ballet (since 1990 Director of the Vereinigte Bühnen, Graz), to recreate and teach several of her dances to specially selected dancers of the Vienna State Opera Ballet for performances at his Viennese International Dance Festival, Tanz '90, and at the Vienna State Opera House.

A live study of Bodenwieser's movements and style was given at Sadler's Wells and a Study-day/Recital arranged with the support of the Austrian Institute, London and the Dance Research Society. Marialuise Jaska, a principal dancer with the Vienna State Opera Ballet, danced *The Sphinx* and *The Mermaid* (Bodenwieser) and *Wein, Weib und Gesang* (Wiesenthal). Classes were also given at the Royal Ballet School (White Lodge), Universities of Surrey and Middlesex, and colleges.

In 1995 the teaching, to the students of the Bruckner Konservatorium, of Bodenwieser movements and the reconstruction of the dance "Terror" from Bodenwieser's trilogy *The Masks of Lucifer* was completed. These were to be included in Esther Linley's production of *Tänze der Verfemten* (*Dances of the Banished*) at Linz and in Tanz '96, Vienna.

As I owe so much to Frau Gerty, it is very gratifying to have been able to perform her dances with Evelyn Ippen in many countries and give illustrated lectures with videos throughout Great Britain and Ireland, and in Salzburg and Vienna.

[At the time of her death, Bettina Vernon had received invitations from Moscow and Poland – Ed.]

Tänze der Verfemten (Dances of the Banished)

[From a text by Andrea Amort[11] in *Tanzdrama*, the Israeli dance quarterly, September 1995.]

A logically formed jigsaw in the shape of a "new-old" dance was solved at the end of a journey through the history of Austrian *Ausdruckstanz* and its present perceptions.

The première of *Dances of the Banished* on 21 April 1995 at the Linz Posthof Theater was not only indicative of the preceding research into what Viennese *Ausdruckstanz* of the thirties and during the time of National Socialism might have been and what sort of ranking it might have had, but also demonstrated the way a choreographer of today manages to deal with this heritage. Most importantly of all, it presented what has been remembered of supposedly authentic material of those choreographers, male and female, who were in the Resistance movement during Nazi times, or had been forced to emigrate.

Since 1977, on the initiative of Viennese dance historians Gunhild Schüller and Alfred Oberzaucher, as well as by Gerhard Brunner, Director

TANZ'90

Sonntag, 11. März, 19.00 Uhr
Sonntag, 11. März, 21.30 Uhr

Ballett der Wiener Staatsoper
Tänze von Gertrud Bodenwieser

Rekonstruktion: Bettina Vernon und Evelyn Ippen
Am Klavier: Winfried van den Hove

Sonnenuntergang (1934)
Musik: Karl Weigl
Es tanzen: Ilonja Dierl, Ingrid Littmann, Erika Nowak, Elisabeth Schüller, Rebecca White, Kira von Zierotin

Nixe (1939)
Musik: Frédéric Chopin
Es tanzt: Marialuise Jaska

Dämon Maschine (1924)
Musik: Lisa Maria Mayer
Es tanzen: Christian Rovny, Ingrid Littmann, Erika Nowak, Elisabeth Schüller, Kira von Zierotin

Sphinx (1940)
Musik: Marcel Lorber
Es tanzt: Marialuise Jaska

Caprice viennois (1943)
Musik: Fritz Kreisler
Es tanzen: Ilonja Dierl, Erika Nowak, Elisabeth Schüller, Rebecca White, Kira von Zierotin

Kibbutz Contemporary Dance Company

Des Dichters Traum (1943)
Choreographie: Gertrud Kraus
Musik: Franz Schubert
Rekonstruktion: Naomi Aleskovsky

Es tanzt: Ensemble

Ballett der Wiener Staatsoper Tanzgestaltungen von Rosalia Chladek

Rekonstruktionen: Rosalia Chladek
Am Klavier: Winfried van den Hove

Aus der Erzengel-Suite: Luzifer (1938)
Es tanzt: Harmen Tromp

19.00 Uhr:
Jeanne d'Arc (1934)
Das Landmädchen Johanna
Berufung – Visionen des Kampfes, Sieges und der Niederlage
Die gefangene Johanna
Erinnerung – Visionen des Gerichtes –
Begnadung
Musik: Erwin Neuber
Es tanzt: Marialuise Jaska

21.30 Uhr:
Kameliendame (1943)
Die Vielgeliebte – Die Verlassene – Die Verlöschende
Musik: Frédéric Chopin
Es tanzt: Elisabeth Stelzer

Kostüme des Balletts der Wiener Staatsoper in Anlehnung an die ursprünglichen Entwürfe:
Edith Pfitzner (Tänze von Gertrud Bodenwieser), Karin Hemmelmayr-Zölß (Tanzgestaltuหgen von Rosalia Chladek)
Originalkostüm der „Kameliendame": Erni Kniepert

36 Program of five Bodenwieser dances performed at the International Dance Festival, Tanz '90, and at the Vienna State Opera House for the first time. Reconstructed and directed by Bettina Vernon and Evelyn Ippen, 1989/90, at the invitation of Dr Gerhard Brunner, Artistic Director Tanz '90 and Director of the Vienna State Opera Ballet (since 1990 Director of the Vereinigte Bühnen, Graz).

37 *Sunset.* Bodenwieser was inspired by the national emblem, the sun, when visiting Japan in 1934. Reconstructed by Bettina Vernon and Evelyn Ippen, 1989/90. Photo: Josef Düport, Vienna.

38 *Demon Machine.* Choreographed 1924. Reconstructed with dancers of the Vienna State Opera Ballet 1989/90 for performances at the Vienna State Opera House and Tanz '90. Photo: Josef Düport, Vienna.

39 *Caprice Viennois.* Choreographed 1943 to Fritz Kreisler's Opus No 2 in memory of Vienna (Kreisler was a personal friend of Bodenwieser). Reconstructed by Bettina Vernon and Evelyn Ippen 1989/90 with dancers of the Vienna State Opera Ballet for Tanz '90 and performances at the Vienna State Opera House. 1989/90. Photo: Josef Düport, Vienna.

THE AUSTRIAN INSTITUTE LONDON
and
THE SOCIETY FOR DANCE RESEARCH
request the pleasure of your company at

a study day/recital

THE VIENNESE SCHOOL
OF FREE EXPRESSIVE DANCE
GRETE WIESENTHAL
AND GERTRUD BODENWIESER
with the participation of

MARIA LUISE JASKA
principal dancer with the VIENNA STATE OPERA BALLET

on Saturday 24 April 1993, beginning at 12 for 12.15 pm

Institut Francais, 17 Queensberry Place, London SW7

Speakers will include:
BETTINA VERNON and EVELYN IPPEN, former principal dancers with the
Bodenwieser Ballet
CLEMENT CRISP, dance critic of the Financial Times
MICHAEL HUXLEY, Acting Head of Performing Arts, De Montfort
University
and CHARLOTTE PURKIS, Lecturer in Music and the Arts in Performance
at the University of Southampton

Dr LESLIE MOORHOUSE will accompany Ms Jaska on the Piano

RSVP (Acceptances only)

40 Viennese School of Free Expressive Dance study day / recital. Arranged by
Andrée Grau and Bettina Vernon, 1993. Presented by the Austrian Institute
London and the Society for Dance Research.

PROGRAMME

12.15   Dr Andrée Grau: Welcome and Introduction to the Day

12.20   Michael Huxley: title to be announced

12.50   Bettina Vernon: **My two famous teachers: Grete Wiesenthal and Gertrud Bodenwieser**

13.30   **LUNCHBREAK**

14.30   Charlotte Purkis: **Dance, music and ideas in turn-of-the-century Vienna**

15.00   Bettina Vernon and Evelyn Ippen, in conversation with Clement Crisp

15.30   **TEA**

RECITAL
(16.00-17.00)

The dance items will be introduced by Bettina Vernon, Evelyn Ippen and Clement Crisp

1   WEIN, WEIB UND GESANG   Maria Luise Jaska
    Choreography G Wiesenthal 1922, Music J Strauss,
    reconstructed by Vilma Kostka and Erika Kniza

2   TRITSCH-TRATSCH POLKA   Dr Leslie Moorhouse
    J Strauss

3   SPHINX   Maria Luise Jaska
    Choreography G Bodenwieser 1939, Music M Lorber,
    reconstructed by Evelyn Ippen and Bettina Vernon 1990

4   TALES FROM THE VIENNA WOODS   Dr Leslie Moorhouse
    J Strauss, L Moorhouse

5   THE MERMAID   Maria Luise Jaska
    Choreography G Bodenwieser 1938, Music F Chopin,
    reconstructed by Bettina Vernon and Evelyn Ippen 1990

Tänze der Verfemten

Regie & Choreographie **Esther Linley**

Bühne **Christian Weininger**

Licht **Christian Weißkircher**

Dramaturgische Mitarbeit **Andrea Amort**

Historische Beratung **Alfred Oberzaucher**

Rekonstruierte Choreographien von

Hanna Berger- einstudiert von **Ottilie Mitterhuber**

Gertrud Bodenwieser- einstudiert von **Bettina Vernon** und **Evelyn Ippen**

Andrei Jerschik- einstudiert vom **Choreographen**

Am Klavier **Leslie Moorhouse**

Es tanzen **Harmen Tromp, Bob Curtis, Esther Koller** sowie
**Nadine Duda, Angela Cooper, Sabile Rasiti, Dolores Hulan, Andrea Müller,
Sabine Roitner, Elfriede Schützender, Michaela Grimus, Karin Koniarek,
Ursula Knapp, Sandra Stöllinger, Barbara Motschiunik,
Michaela Schweighofer, Barbara Mülleder, Sandra Hofstötter,
Angelika Türschel, Marie Rose Misek, Nomathemba Mzimela,
Philipp Stummer** und **Thomas Hanslmaier**

Musik **Rachmaninov, Debussy, Mussorgsky, Ravel, Verdi, Strauß, Brahms,
Dvorak, Fast Forward, Austral Voices, Richard Tauber, Fatima Miranda,
Boris Kovac**

Uraufgeführt am 21. April 1995
im Rahmen der Kontraste-Tage im Posthof Linz.

────────────►   story: ankunft in südamerika.... „Exercise an der Stange" [Bodenwieser]....„Slavonic Dance"

[Bodenwieser] .... news from home.....where are the children....„Narrow and wide [dreamy and romantic",

Bodenwieser]....laufen....tanzen ist überleben....the night of departure....„Four-Corner-Step" [melancholic and

depressed, Bodenwieser]....„Swinging" [Bodenwieser]....frieden ist ein kaffeehaus.... „The Four-Corner-Step"

[happy, joyful Viennese mood, Bodenwieser]...no going back..... „Terror" [Bodenwieser]....doch ein neuer

anfang.... „Die Unbekannte aus der Seine" [Berger]....even if we were to tell it.... „Der Mensch im Wahn"

[Jerschik]....the chase.... ankunft in....

Ein Wesenszug des ausgehenden 20. Jahrhunderts ist die penible Aufarbeitung der Geschichte: um Fragen

der (künstlerischen und politischen) Identität zu klären. Auch die flüchtigste aller Künste, den Tanz, hat die Frage nach

seinem Bestand und seinem „woher" erfaßt.

In Österreich wird seit 1977 (vor allem durch die Initiative von Gerhard Brunner) versucht, zu bewahren, was

an choreographischem Erbe in Resten vorhanden ist: von Grete Wiesenthal, Gertrud Kraus,

Gertrud Bodenwieser und Rosalia Chladek, die 90jährig 1995 starb. Augenscheinlich wurde

seither die reiche Tradition des (nichtklassischen) Expressionismus in all seinen Facetten, der in den 20er und

30er Jahren Mitteleuropa beherrschte. Es war das nationalsozialistische Regime, das viele der (jüdischen)

Tänzer-Choreographen flüchten machte, andere zur Resignation zwang.

Die „Tänze der Verfemten" zeigen anders als bisher nicht eine Folge von historischen

Rekonstruktionen, sondern weben die wertvollen Spuren politisch verfolgter Choreographen in ein

zeitgenössisches Netz zum Thema Verlust des Menschseins ein.

Das alte Kunst-Material, das sowohl den Zeitgeschmack wie die Aussagekraft des vergangenen Ausdrucks-

tanzes lebendig heraufbeschwört, wurde so direkt als möglich an die junge Generation weitergegeben.

Bettina Vernon, die kurz nach der Linzer Premiere der „Tänze der Verfemten" 1995 in

London starb und Evelyn Ippen haben (als ehemalige Schülerinnen) Beispiele aus Gertrud Bodenwiesers

Werk einstudiert. Andrei Jerschik, der auch Partner von Bodenwieser war, hat sein Solo

„Mensch im Wahn" direkt auf den in Rekonstruktionen (vor allem von Rosalia Chladek)

erfahrenen Harmen Tromp übertragen. Und Ottilie Mitterhuber gab (als ehemalige Schülerin)

von Hanna Berger deren Tanz „Die Unbekannte aus der Seine" weiter.

Auf der Spurensuche nach künstlerischer Identität sind sämtliche für die „Tänze der Verfemten"

aufgefundenen Bewegungs-Materialien bisher weitgehend unbekannt gewesen.   *Andrea Amort*

41 Program of *Tänze der Verfemten* (*Dances of the Banished*), Tanz '96, Vienna. Bodenwieser dances taught by Bettina Vernon and Evelyn Ippen. At the piano: Leslie Moorhouse, concert pianist, composer and pianist with Marcel Lorber for *Ballet for Two* and subsequent ventures with Bettina Vernon and Evelyn Ippen until the reconstruction of Bodenwieser dances for *Tänze der Verfemten* which he accompanied at Linz and Tanz '96 Vienna performances.

of the Graz Theaters and manager of the Tanz-Biennale, as much as possible of the preserved oeuvre of *Ausdruckstanz* has been kept alive through being performed: works by Grete Wiesenthal, by Rosalia Chladek, as well as by choreographers who emigrated like Gertrud Bodenwieser and Gertrud Kraus. The idea of the Brucknerhaus Linz to commission *Dances of the Banished* arose in talks between Esther Linley,[12] Andrea Amort and Alfred Oberzaucher.

The theme of the Linz "Days of Contrast" (18–22 April 1995), "50 Years after the End of World War II", gave Esther Linley the impulse to mount works, as yet unknown, from the oeuvre of ostracized choreographers, set into the framework of a dramaturgically contemporary production. Freelance dancers Esther Koller, Bob Curtis and Harmen Tromp, as well as students of the Bruckner Konservatorium, were to be the performers. Two of Gertrud Bodenwieser's Viennese former students, Bettina Vernon and Evelyn Ippen, came to Linz several times to stage dances and exercises by their onetime teacher. In 1938 Bodenwieser, being Jewish, had to emigrate first to France and later to Australia. The pieces chosen demonstrate the stylistic variety and colorfulness of Bodenwieser's expressionism: "Terror" (see Choreochronicle), reconstructed here for the first time (first performance: Vienna 1936, a part of the dance-drama *The Masks of Lucifer*, ch: Bodenwieser; music: M. Lorber), turned out to be a clearly constructed, strikingly compact tragedy of a family driven to death through terror. In the opening scene the family is shown huddled together on the floor. Through dance techniques and expressive gestures the individual members of the family: the father trying to resist; the mother begging for mercy; the children magically attracted towards terror; slowly evolve. In a quadrangle of firm steps the figure of terror closes in on the family. In an atmosphere of latent anti-Semitism, which finally became law in Austria through the *Anschluss* of 1938, Bodenwieser's ballet might have contributed towards a raised alertness. Again and again her oeuvre is interwoven with works of a socially critical context (like *Demon Machine*). The other dance studies, amongst them excerpts of the exercise at the barre as taught by Bodenwieser during the thirties at the Vienna Music Academy, show her preference (perhaps shared with Wiesenthal) for swinging movements and turns, always executed in two different moods. Amongst them was also the "Four Corner Step", an effective paraphrase of the waltz-step, executed "in a happy joyful Viennese mood" and/or "a melancholic and depressed mood". Bettina Vernon, who in numerous lectures preserved Bodenwieser's heritage in London, asserted that Sir Frederick Ashton is said to have taken great interest in the four corner step.

Completely unknown up to now has been the personal style of the Viennese Hanna Berger (1910–1962), born in Vienna. At the age of 19 she went to Berlin to dance with Mary Wigman's ensemble, was arrested in the autumn of 1942 for being a member of the communist resistance movement Rote Kapelle, and was kept prisoner in the Oranienburg concentration camp until 1945. Berger taught at the dance department of the Vienna Music Academy up to 1952. She formed her own Kammertanztruppe (Chamber dance company), probably around 1954, and, besides her own works, also performed choreographies by Wiesenthal. Paul Kont was sometimes procured as composer. In East Berlin she worked with the eminent director Walter Felsenstein (Janáček's *Cunning Little Vixen*) and also with the mime Marcel Marceau on various projects. Her former student and later pedagogue Ottilie Mitterhuber, now living in Vienna, has reconstructed the solo *The Unknown from the Seine* (first performance 1942, music Debussy) for the young Esther Koller: in a long dress, the eyes fixed to the ground, the woman slowly drowns, groping cautiously with widespread arms.

A solo piece was recreated as an example of the numerous creations of Andrei Jerschik, a 93-year old Viennese now living in Linz. Jerschik was one of the most sought-after expressionist dancers of the thirties. During the Nazi regime he had been on the run because of his anti-fascist attitude.

It was Esther Linley's task to create a context and a frame for the dances. Her foremost concern was to present on stage human beings of today who, faced with the menace of neo-fascism, are again experiencing terror and fear, having been overtaken by the past-demonstrating that we still have a lot to learn from history.

Dances Choreographed by Bettina Vernon and Evelyn Ippen in the Bodenwieser Style

1940	*Czechoslovakian Polka*	Weinberger
	*Death and the Maiden**	Schubert
1941	*Dreams**	—
	Contrast	Brahms
1942	*Tales from the Vienna Woods*	Johann Strauss
	L'Aiglon	Haydn, Mozart
	Drunk with Happiness	Mozart
	Delirious Fever	Mozart
	Conscience	Lorber
	Bonds of Harmony	Brahms
	Augustin	Viennese Melodies – Lorber
	Poldenice (Mid-day Witch)	Dvořák
	Snowman's Prank	Lorber
	Weather House	Lorber
	Largo and Slavonic Dance	Dvořák
	Cleopatra	Lorber
	See no Evil, Hear no Evil, Speak no Evil	Lorber
	Resignation	Viennese Melodies
1943	*Overture to Die Fledermaus*	Johann Strauss
	Wild Flight	Lorber

*These two dances were performed in the Bodenwieser Ballet.

1944	*Voices of Spring*	Johann Strauss
	Diana	Richard Strauss
	Presentation of the Silver Rose –	
	Der Rosenkavalier (*The Knight*	
	of the Rose)	Richard Strauss
1945	*Lights on*	Popular Melodies

Notes

1. Danzer was a family name.
2. "One of the best achievements was *Fast zu Keck*. Theory and technique exemplarily executed by the graceful, lively and spirited ballerina Lanzer [Vernon]."
3. Originally known as *Meluse* when composed in Austria.
4. See plate 9 on pages 58 and 59.
5. A Viennese term of endearment.
6. It is believed to be unusual for Bodenwieser to produce a whole ballet on points. [Ed.]
7. Extracted from *Wie weit ist Wien?* (*How far is Vienna?*) Latin America as Exile for Austrian writers and artists by Alisa Douer and Ursula Schreiber (ed.) and *Collaboration* by Edith Blaschitz. Editorial Picus, Vienna, 1995. Extract and translation provided by Claire H. de Robilant.
8. Male guest artists were Ronnie Curran, Robert Harrold and Colin Paterick.
9. Walter Foster OBE, who retired in 1990 as General Secretary of the Anglo-Austrian Society, accompanied Bettina Vernon and Evelyn Ippen on many of their early tours of the UK.
10. Extract from the "50 years, Anglo-Austrian Society – 1942–1992" publication *"If music be the food of love … play on"*.
11. Andrea Amort: dance journalist, lecturer and dramaturge.
12. The English dancer and choreographer Esther Linley, formerly with the Tanztheater Wien, has been director of the department for dance education at the Bruckner Konservatorium since 1993, and in that capacity has also been responsible for the reform of contemporary dance education at this institution.

15

LEARNING – AN EXHILARATION AND A JOY

Innes Murdoch

It is hard to believe that we wore hats everywhere in 1939. Even more surprising is that we wore them to dancing classes, as a matter of course! But all that is a very long time ago, when life was much more formal. Times change, but memory lingers.

I had started classical ballet training as a child in Sydney, absorbing it very easily. Coordination came with no effort. But sadly, what may have been a mainstream incentive was interrupted when my father was transferred to Melbourne and I was sent to a country boarding school. No more ballet classes ... .

Years later, while I was finishing my schooling in England and Europe, my father died in France. My mother and I found ourselves temporarily under the wing of a distant cousin, living in Paris – Maude Dunlop, with her children, Bonar and Shona.

The family had been living in Vienna where Shona had been studying Modern Dance with a Gertrud Bodenwieser, but, because of the political situation, they had left Vienna. They were now in Paris where Shona was continuing her dance training. I remember well her showing us a very energetic Russian dance that she had just been taught; it left her breathless and me full of admiration!

It was in March 1938, I think, for I remember listening to the Radio about the *Anschluss*, and Major Campbell (later to become Shona's step-father) looking extremely grave, saying that the situation was serious indeed. It all wafted over my head.

My mother and I left shortly afterwards, she, returning to Australia, I , to England to finish my schooling until 1939, when I, too, returned before the outbreak of war.

Meanwhile, the tumult in Europe had forced many to flee; Gertrud Bodenwieser, together with her pianist Marcel Lorber and her Dance group, had managed to escape to Colombia, South America. They hoped to establish a new school there at Bogotá, but it proved to be unfeasible. Shona, now a member of the Group, with the help of her family managed to obtain permission for Bodenwieser and Marcel to live in New Zealand. It was not to be for long, however, for it was decided that the population of New Zealand was not large enough to support a Modern Dance School. Sydney, Australia, was thought to be a better option, so the migration continued to Sydney. There, fortunately, Bodenwieser managed to unite with some of her leading dancers who had been on tour in New York and had, subsequently, gained permission to live in Australia. An amazing piece of good fortune!

I'm not sure who arrived in Sydney first: Shona from New Zealand, or me from England; however, the mothers were in touch. In no time I met Shona again, who was bubbling over with the excitement of establishing a new Dance School.

I was not aware of the importance of Bodenwieser at this stage, nor did I know anything about modern dance, and precious little about classical ballet! Australia was a delightful child-country in those days, and very little of the cultural life of Europe reached her shores. I didn't have a chance to say 'No', however, when Shona said that I must join the newly-formed dance classes. She was recruiting with all the zeal of the converted. In no time she had me in the dance studio, located on top of a restaurant in King Street, right in the heart of the city. This was in August 1940.

It was a wonderfully large, airy room, flooded with sunlight and fully carpeted. The owner of the restaurant, Vere Mathews, had seen a demonstration given by the Bodenwieser group and was captivated. She, herself, also had her own School of Physical Exercise in this studio, and, realising the importance of this new style of movement, went out of her way to help Bodenwieser establish herself. Bodenwieser had the use of this lovely studio until she was able to find a suitable place entirely for her own work.

I remember very little about the actual first class, but I do vividly remember how quickly I became engrossed. Temperamentally, it was exactly right. Within weeks I was attending classes daily, becoming really eager to do well, and watching every detail demonstrated by the experienced girls from Vienna who assisted Bodenwieser at every class. Emmy Taussig, Evelyn Ippen and Bettina Vernon were closest to me and each gave unstintingly of their help and encouragement.

We wore short black tunics with full flowing sleeves of georgette in the color of our choice. Those sleeves, together with our shoulder-length hair, were admirable complements with which to express mood or movement, and the short tunics and our bare feet gave us every freedom to illustrate shade and meaning.

Little Frau Gerty! She wasn't very tall. What I remember most vividly are those sparkling brown eyes with the quizzical expression. I can see the jet-black hair, tightly drawn back into a chignon, the white blouse, topped by the loose black bib trousers, the neat black ballet

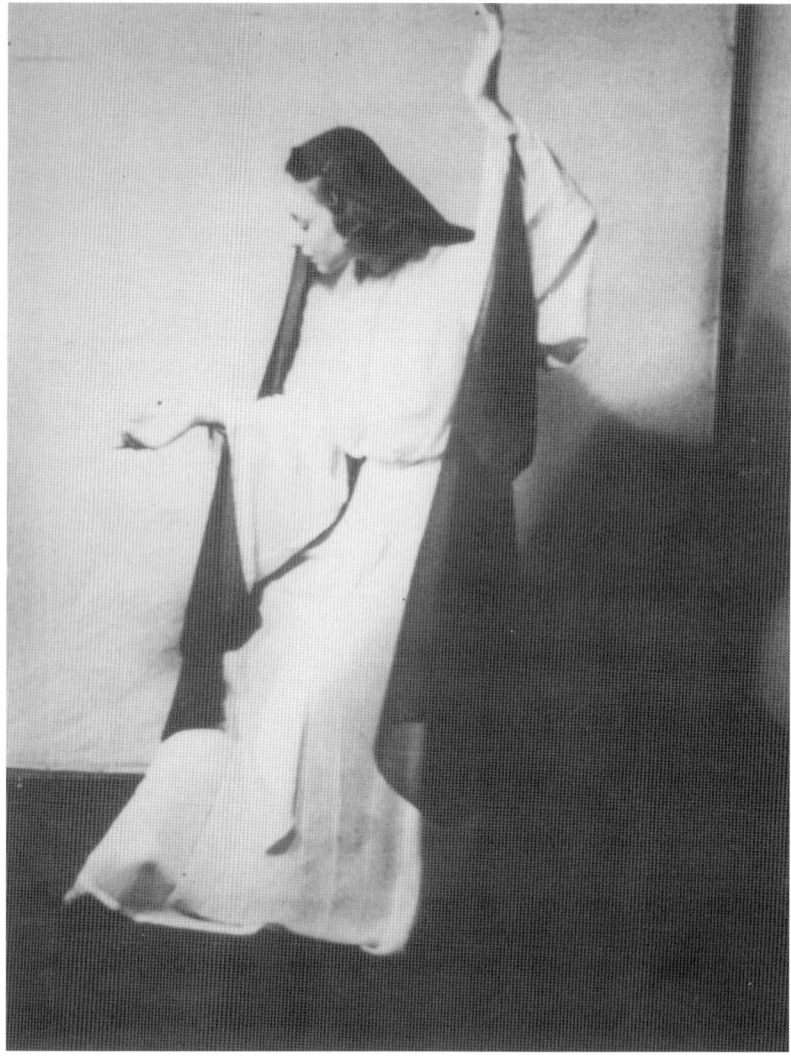

42 *Maria's Annunciation.* Innes Murdoch, the first Australian to be given a leading part in the Bodenwieser Ballet. Photo: Leica-Flash, Sydney, 1941.

shoes. All of her movements were harmonious; even her normal walk seemed to flow.

Unbeknown to me at the time, Bodenwieser was to become a lasting influence in my life. She is one of the few people I remember with love and appreciation for all that she gave us.

It began, of course, with the physical: the daily classes, starting with a semi-classical warm-up; with limbering exercises at the barre, often incorporating a theme which would be developed during the class (which nearly always finished with an improvisation). Systematically, every part of the body would be used, developing strength, suppleness, elasticity, grace, endurance and, most importantly, imagination. Creative interpretation of movement played a very big part in our training. We'd emerge from a class with an incredible sense of well-being and fulfilment – complete – content.

Marcel Lorber was Bodenwieser's wonderful pianist. He had been with her in Vienna, and added much to the enrichment of the classes and our musical experience. Through Marcel we unconsciously learnt a great deal about music and musical appreciation.

With a light step and wicked smile, the jaunty Marcel, felt hat at a rakish angle, would sweep into the studio on the hour. His magical touch inspired us all. How lucky we were! It was still there just a few years ago. Here in London. I was with Marcel while he was trying out a piano that a friend wanted to buy. Marcel sat down and played *The Blue Danube*, the epitome of all Viennese waltzes. The sheer sensitivity of it again produced a tremor of excitement and reduced me to tears of nostalgia!

After the war, Marcel went on tour to Japan and thence to England with Evelyn and Bettina. Dory Stern, also from Vienna, and a great admirer of Bodenwieser, later took Marcel's place. She admirably replaced him, but my training was mostly done in the days of Marcel, so I remember him more clearly.

Before very long, Bodenwieser had found a suitable studio for herself on Pitt Street, where she was able to work more fully. Not having an established school from which to select future dancers for the group, she had to work with what she had; that included the first students in Australia. We were especially encouraged when two girls from Europe (Katya and Katrine) left the group to marry. Edith Shorter (Czech?), Stella Zahara (New Zealander), Stella Simpson (English) and I (Australian) were the first to join the group and we became truly dedicated. Eileen Cramer (Australian) and others joined shortly after.

At about this time it was the students' custom to go to a Coffee House after class for a light meal. Boddy (Frau Gerty) often came with us, and there began the first of the analytical and philosophical discussions. It was a radical change from the type of conversation normal for a young Australian. Bodenwieser was interested not only in our dancing abilities, but felt that to understand fully the depth of her work, it was necessary for us to develop intellectually. She took us into the most interesting by-ways, and I shall never forget the enlightening moment when

I perceived that everything was relative! Trite now, but quite a revelation then and a thought which helped me to put things into a better perspective. On another occasion we were discussing ability and talent. Bodenwieser reflected upon what was, perhaps, most pertinent. She wondered how much great talent fell by the wayside through the force of circumstances.

Before long, Bodenwieser established more formal classes for us: Theory and History of Physical Education; History of Dance (and the periods in which it developed); Knowledge of various systems of Physical Education; Physiology, Anatomy and Biology; History and Appreciation of Music. In greater depth we studied the four greatest 19th-century influences on Modern Dance: Bess Mensendieck, Delsarte, Dalcroze, Laban, and, of course, in the 20th century, Isadora Duncan, the true mother of Modern Dance.

Gradually, especially amongst the Central European migrants who had escaped their homelands, Bodenwieser became more widely known and appreciated, but work was not available to support the group members as it had been in Europe. Most of the dancers started teaching their own classes. Shona became Bodenwieser's assistant (mainly on Sydney's North Shore); Emmy and another student (Ena Noel) taught in the Eastern suburbs; Bettina and Evelyn and Emmy had their own schools and assisted Bodenwieser with the growing number of Australian students in her studio.

It being wartime, there were many requests for fund raising charity performances. Expenses only were paid, but it was a good means of gaining recognition. Soon, I, too, started having small parts. The first exciting evening was at the Ballet Festival, held at the Minerva Theater in aid of the Red Cross in March 1941, and my first solo dance, *Maria's Annunciation* (Bach/Gounod), was choreographed for me in September 1941.

The New South Wales State Conservatorium of Music was the main venue for Music, Opera and Dance Recitals at that time. It was long before the famous Opera House was built. We students took delight in being asked to appear in the various operas; *Tales of Hoffmann* and *Don Giovanni* remain foremost in my memory, especially the occasion when I appeared on stage bare-footed but dressed in 18th-century satin and lace finery! I had forgotten to bring the pink ballet slippers. Poor Frau Gerty – I'll never forget her ire at what I thought then a very slight misdemeanor.

And another ghastly moment occurred towards the close of a performance of *Cain and Abel* in which Bodenwieser herself had taken part. She had changed from her costume into a long, black evening gown in which to take the end-of-recital applause, and asked me to zip up the back of this dress. We were all on the *qui vive* and in my hurry I caught her flesh in the zipper! Absolute horror! I had to unzip the skin and, of course, it bled – just before her entry on stage. It was a good thing that the dress was black. She had a lot to put up with, with all these inexperienced girls, but no doubt their youth and enthusiasm helped somewhat to alleviate her personal anguish at what was going on in Europe and, in particular, to her husband.

The daily classes punctuated our lives; it was rare to miss one. Besides those given by Bodenwieser, Evelyn started a jumping class for us, Bettina a waltz class. Both were invaluable and without doubt increased our competence.

Can you imagine, therefore, the moment of excitement when Emmy and Evelyn came up and told me that I had been chosen to fill in for – was it Katya? Anyway, they needed a fifth dancer for that very night's performance of *The Slavonic Dance*. They would teach it to me that lunch hour. Never have I concentrated so hard, or learnt any subsequent dance so quickly! My goodness, I can still smell the greasepaint on that Slavonic costume, a flamboyant creation by Evelyn: red bodice with a long, swirling skirt; long gathered white sleeves; a swathe of large appliqué flowers trailing from arm to hem. It was 24 May 1942. My first appearance as a real member of the group; Katya later sold me her Slavonic dress and it became a most treasured possession. The role of Truth in *The Pilgrimage of Truth* was given to me in 1943.

Beside the Bodenwieser Dance Group, there were several other classical ballet people working at the time, notably, Edouard Borovansky (who subsequently opened his school in Melbourne) and Helene Kirsova, who formed a company in Sydney. These rival groups were always of great interest to us as classical ballet, better known to Australian audiences, had the edge of public approval. We were always interested in learning more about the classical dancers and sometimes we encountered one another at Repins Coffee Shop, opposite our former Studio in King Street. On one historic occasion, not even having enough money for *two* cups of coffee, Eileen Cramer ordered one, and I a glass of water to enable us to sit and chat! We ate the sugar lumps on the table . . . .

At that time Eileen was living in some very Bohemian place in a very old house near Hunter Street which has since been demolished. The communal washing area was in an open courtyard, and the wash-trough a long dented tin affair. Those living there even shared the one bar of soap and slid it along the trough to one another as they made their ablutions. They were fun years, when the sun always seemed to shine, and the only irritant was the occasional splinter that we picked up in our bare feet from the wooden floor of the studio.

Since it was war time, of course, and we were penurious to boot, we were not able to buy many new clothes, but this problem was easily solved! We bought and sold from each other. Eileen, I remember, bought my famous Lapin (ordinary rabbit) fur coat and wore it until the fur practically dropped off. I fear that we Antipodeans were an odd lot to Bodenwieser who was brought up in the twilight years of the formal Hapsburg reign. It was a far cry from Vienna and the Emperor Franz Josef, and her own sheltered upbringing did not equip her for easy survival in a tougher world.

Early in my years of friendship with her I even had to show her how to make toast! She had hardly entered a kitchen in her life, but subsequently learnt how to entertain her bridge partners when they came, on occasion, to play at the studio. The studio really was her home; certainly it was the center of her life, as it was ours, and we lived in easy communication.

I can see her now, cleansing her face with lanolin and leaving the residue on as a base. I can see her dressing after a class, fixing her famous black net veil, tightly drawn under the chin and up, over the small black hat. I can hear her pretty accented voice instructing us in class. We very soon learnt to understand "Viennese-English", and I regret enormously now not having had the wit to grab such a wonderful chance of learning German, as well as dancing. The girls from Europe, together with Frau Gerty, always spoke German amongst themselves. It became commonplace to our ears, but we were not motivated to learn it. Languages other than English were of little practical value in a land so far from Europe.

Towards the end of 1946, Stella Zahara and I decided to try a little choreography for ourselves. With the help of another excellent pianist, Kurt Herweg, we arranged a program which we took on tour to six centers in New South Wales, amongst them Canberra, where I met my future husband. Bodenwieser was not happy about this, but I think that inwardly she was pleased that two of her raw students had been able to progress so far as to be able to present a duo recital. We were the first of the Australian students to form an independent dance team. It was fun and taught us a great deal, but it was not a roaring financial success! What we were able to do was entirely due to the wonderful training that we were given by Bodenwieser.

Few people have had the good fortune to meet such a remarkable woman at the right moment in their lives; her influence on me was, and is still, profound. I am who I am today because of what Bodenwieser brought with her from Europe and imparted to those of us who studied with her. None of us remained 'Australian' in the narrow sense of the word. Our world opened out to encompass the heritage and culture of Europe, a world rich indeed, which continues to absorb those who are aware of the joy of learning.

I married not long afterwards and of necessity our lives drifted along other channels. She visited me once, not long after my first child was born, and I remember her picking up one tiny foot, examining it minutely. "How wonderfully beautiful it is,"she mused, "and how ugly man can make them later on!"

The last time that I saw her was in her bed, at St Luke's Hospital. She had had a heart attack. The long, black hair was loose around her shoulders. It was unreal to see her stricken and tears welled from my eyes. I think that at that moment she realised that we really cared, that we really loved her.

I hope that that knowledge brought her a little comfort.

26 September 1992

16

VISION

Coralie Hinkley

She made the nature of dance visible.[1]

I became completely absorbed in the views of modern dance, and responded passionately to the vision, philosophy, principles and language of movement expressed by Gertrud Bodenwieser.

We do not ask of our generation to express themselves in the way of those of past generations...
The idea of the new dance is that it has taken up relationship with the great stream of modern living, choosing its topics not only from a fancy world of lightness and charm... but a world full of problems and strife, great ideas and development; the modern dance does not wish to be only amusing and entertaining; it aims to be stirring, exciting, and thought provoking. That is the ideal of any real art.[2]

To me it was a never-ending source of wonder, of beauty, both visual and spiritual.
Having studied, danced, performed, taught and created for many years within the modern dance technique of Gertrud Bodenwieser (with 'Madame' as my teacher and choreographer), I came to know the powerful energy of the body in dance, to assimilate, communicate and love her way-of-dance in all its aspects of expressive insight.
This art form presented itself with subtlety and power from the most open spontaneous movement to the smallest and delicate, presenting itself in classwork, studio dance and theater performances as a visionary and powerful art: through qualities of movement, dynamics, emotions – feelings, musicality and form in solo dance, group dances, dance-dramas in her own original choreographic style.
The demands of her technique embraced the circle, wave, arc, spiral – never static – always fluid – never-ending gradations of flow, rhythms, designs, expressions, with the breath as the *impulse* for the surge of dance.
To be part of the Modern Dance of Gertrud Bodenwieser meant a way of giving oneself, one's inner and outer being, to a range of moods,

expressions, changes of feeling, sensitivities, characterisations, through the expressive dance forms of the movement and insight of her technique and art, of her creative choreographic use of the body–mind–spirit.

Our lyrical or dramatic qualities were projected through the fluidity of unfolding movement from the center of breath out to the extremities.

The rise and fall of the breath, phrasing of the movement sequences, musical awareness and connections, whether in the symmetry of the dance lines or the conflict of the unequal, achieved special qualities of texture and form, depth, meaning.

Gertrud Bodenwieser's vision-in-dance of *the human condition*, the message, universal. This was communicated through her choreographic art and subsequently performed by the ensemble of dancers … representing the depths of Flow as the body uncurled in the Back Wave … the vitality of joyousness in the *Slavonic Dance* with five dancers swirling in a pulse of movement – exuberant, expansive – a physical 'dynamic' of turns, jumps, kicks, bends … or hollowing out of the body shape, concave, as three dancers, 'whose souls are oppressed', trudge heavy-footed in the shape of *A Cart drawn by Man* – the pull of movement tensions was inward, downward, or thrust upward in gestures that protested, challenging oppression … in *Dance of Remorse*, falls, knee crawls, accentuated my mode of earth-bound suffering in *The Grecian Suite*.

We, the dance children of Gertrud Bodenwieser, attended classes in her studio at 210 Pitt Street, Sydney, between the years 1942 and 1957. We were her students, her dancers, and for many of us the beginning of this experience was a much treasured part of our formative years.

It was in those classes that Gertrud Bodenwieser imparted to us the principles of her dance technique, when bodies and minds were responsive to the movement that she established through her art form. This inspired a small group of us and we were awakened by a profound *need* to dance. In our bodies and spirit was the lightness of air, the feeling of the earth, the mystery of moon-flowers. She made us aware of the special nature of these qualities, so that we could bring out the feeling and expression that was so much a part of Bodenwieser's approach – a realisation of dance allied to music.

She knew instinctively *how* to bring out each one's individual style, our personal gifts and talents. Her presence was poetic and her wisdom deep.

We were drawn to her, to the nuances of her movement and dance – narratives.

The simplest elements in her dance technique held a surprising delight. For example, one such as *the change of weight* from one side to the other, the body held in a perfect side arc, with the weight transferred

43 *The Wheel of Life*. From top: Coralie Hinkley, Mardi Watchorn, Eileen Cramer. Based on the writings and philosophy of Krishnamurti: from *The Search*. Photo: Margaret Michaelis, Sydney, 1947.

smoothly and effortlessly from one side to the other, the side arc changing with the weight change.

In the dance-drama, *The Insects*, a satire on human behavior, we hovered in shifting flights of movement and vibrating balances; as butterflies fluttering, symbolising the superficial and frivolous in human nature.

In expressing vigor or a color such as *red*, our spontaneous energy was directed into the *daring of the leap*.

The basis of Gertrud Bodenwieser's modern dance *art form* was the circle, based on geometry. "Every movement is a design in space", she said.

Madame embraced the design of the wave, figure of eight and loop. These forms were then metamorphosed into living, breathing elaborations through our' expressive bodies and their parts: arms, fingers, face, head, hair, neck, shoulders, limbs, feet, initiating variations in the configurations of the arc, circle, spiral, tilt, bend, curve.

The source of the dance and our expression from the simplest gesture to the most complex combinations came from *within*.

Some of my favorite movements in my kinetic memory are: a pure opening of the spirit as the leg is lifted back slowly, at the same time the body opening and bending back on the leg, simultaneously arms opening into a circle … ripples of the body – side wave – faster than light.

The classes were limitless in their creativeness. We were given insight into ways to transpose movement, different gradations of flow, dynamics, rhythms, expressions. One could elaborate on a simple movement – design, changing the levels, or shape, uniformity or distortion, a re-vitalizing influence on the original design.

There were moments of great complexity in Bodenwieser's choreography.

In *The Wheel of Life* Mardi Watchorn, Eileen Cramer and I reflected with Madame on the meaning of the philosophy of Krishnamurti, and the form that the dance work would take. The human figures depicted the experiences of life, rhythms of pain and pleasure – caught up in the inevitability of the momentum of The Wheel – *the dance figure of destiny at the center of the turning world*.

Gertrud Bodenwieser's ideas were fresh and innovative, emphasizing different layers of aesthetic approach and understanding applied to time, strength, dynamics, music, rhythms, patterns, harmony, symmetry, opposition, succession, groupings. The fluency of the sense of poetry in her dance together with imaginative vitality led to a richness of theme and texture rather than repetition or automatic predictability. She said "expression is the basis of the soul given through form". I found each class, each choreographic idea, full of wonder. It was a mode of dance which, according to Madame, suited the physicality, personality, and temperament of the Australian.

We, as Australian dancers, responded. We developed a passionate concern and commitment to her, as a great artist of the modern dance, for those values and qualities that she so generously passed on to us.

At the time in Sydney, 1940 onwards, for a few short years, we were inspired by the nucleus of the European dancers of the Bodenwieser Dance Group: Evelyn Ippen, Bettina Vernon, Emmy Taussig and Shona Dunlop (from New Zealand). They shared the beauty of Bodenwieser dance with us as performers and teachers.

Bettina Vernon in the Waltz class instructed us in a kaleidoscope of fluid lines, slow or fast curvings of body movement in her inimitable lyrical style, a delicate balance through the body and limbs, growing out of the breath, music and feeling, arcs of poetic control. Her dance-like gestures were exquisite; her fluency of movement gave a special radiance.

The vigor and technical freedom in the dance of Evelyn Ippen sprang to life in the classes she gave to us on Elevation, (jumping), an explosion of energetic activity.

When Evelyn and Bettina left the Bodenwieser Dance Company, to continue their professional careers overseas, we young Australians who had shown dedication and exceptional promise in modern dance were chosen by Madame to take over some of the roles that Evelyn and Bettina had so beautifully danced and interpreted.

Great works such as *Demon Machine, The Masks of Lucifer, The Pilgrimage of Truth, Cradle Song of Mother Earth, Sunset, Waterlilies, Dance with golden discs, A Cart drawn by Man*, and many others, therefore remained in the repertoire. The new group of Australian dancers developed a unity of effort to a remarkable degree; all were deeply involved in her art form.

Bodenwieser had a special appreciation of our qualities and our responsiveness to her principles – the concepts of her dance as an expressive art form. We took nothing for granted, discovering by loyalty and hard work the deep concern she had for each dancer. "No two individuals are alike" she said. Bodenwieser worked with this conviction in mind. I also believe that this concept is worth saving in a world in which too much emphasis is placed on conformity.

Those of us who were members of the Bodenwieser dance company in Australia shared a common ideal. We were honed by Madame into a fine modern dance group; many of the dancers today still resonate with those expressive ideals. We absorbed and assimilated the aesthetic value of expressiveness. Forms, ideas, musical interpretation, dramatic and lyrical representations in narrative or abstract form, developed our performing, creative and teaching abilities.

I inherited the solo dance of Evelyn Ippen, *The Sphinx*, The Demon in *Demon Machine*, and the demanding role of Lucifer in *The Masks of Lucifer*, among many other roles in the repertoire of her choreographies. One had to find the means of understanding the content, the subtle shading and contrasts in meaning, if one wished to project in the performances.

As a dancer, being part of the artistic experience of her choreographic works also meant growth and development of one's musical sensitivities. These were awakened and guided by Dory Stern,[3] who made us musically aware and preserved the interaction between music and the dance. This relationship was extended as imaginative accompaniment to dance improvisation or interest in a musical composition written for a choreographic idea. The hard work, discipline, sacrifice were unimportant to me; only the responses to the inspiration of Bodenwieser's imagination, her artistic concepts, interpretations and dance forms mattered. Thus I emerged as a dancer in the Bodenwieser style, a member of her company and a teacher in her school.

As a teacher, Gertrud Bodenwieser was always constructive. Each class was a process of growth and development, a joy, a revelation. Our consciousness was heightened by her lively expressive intelligence. She created among the dancers a *need to dance*, to give utterance to her vision. We assimilated Bodenwieser's approach to choreography; the intuitive feeling for composition, the insights into *the predicament of man – his joys and sorrows*. Opportunity was given to us to create movements within the conception of the subject matter or theme.

It was, for me, the first stirring of awareness of creativity.

Fragments of our imagination were threaded through many of the newer choreographies. For instance in *The Life of the Insects*, the dancers as beetles experimented with strange and weird articulations of the limbs, as they moved from place to place, pushing and hoarding possessions. Sharp runs, uneasy pattern changes expressed the aggressive instincts of ants. The dancers flowed through their organic shapes in the cycle of birth, death, re-birth, within the frame of the inevitability of motion in *The Wheel of Life*. The experience of the dance imagery in *Vision*,[4] after one of the etchings of Goya, heightened one's sense of creativity, interpreting Spanish-inspired movement in the changing images of good and evil. The beautiful rich young girl fails to recognize the old hag who is following her begging: "Dios La Perdone; Yera Su Madre"; God forgive her; it was her mother!

As dancers our *creative personality*[5] was brought into focus by Gertrud Bodenwieser, who in her search for truth and beauty could touch the human spirit. That is why I stayed so long.

In the eleven years of dance association with Gertrud Bodenwieser[6] my intuitive mind responded to all her dance situations and their meanings, and I was able, therefore, at a later date, to grasp and understand the techniques and philosophies of the Modern Dance of Martha Graham, Merce Cunningham, Doris Humphrey and Louis Horst,[7] techniques which, although different in viewpoints and approaches, all had the same *essence*: an imaginative richness of material and a search for truth.

In 1958 at the Summer School of Dance, Connecticut College, I invited Doris Humphrey to visit Australia to meet Gertrud Bodenwieser.[8] I felt that they would understand, value and respect each other for their artistic and creative minds. Both had deep human values and had overcome personal suffering to continue their art. Like so many great artists, Madame Bodenwieser always retained the quality of innocence, in a world in which she experienced man's more ignoble instincts.

Lastly, the experiences in dance with Gertrud Bodenwieser heightened my creative awareness contributing to the freeing of imaginative sources so that now I am able to activate the creative energy not only in dance but in the expressiveness of the world – *a new transformation in a creative life*.

Extracts from a letter, dated 3 July 1995, from Coralie Hinkley to Innes Murdoch

... to think of that beautiful dancer – no longer here on earth – my thoughts about Bettina go very far back – not so far back as yours – but nevertheless all the early technique of Madame, which I think was the best time – and how beautifully Bettina interpreted all her parts – her lyrical style, interpretation and technique were flawless ...

I think that everything that she did was exquisite – a real dancer – the beautiful développés, and her seemingly effortless tilts of the body (off centre) – her solos, *The Mermaid*, her part in *Caprice Viennois*, even the braggart in *The Pilgrimage of Truth*, were beautifully done.

I always felt a sense of something missing when E and B left Madame – somehow the lyrical and dramatic quality of Madame's dance was never quite the same again – I don't mean that other dancers were *not* good or even less in dance interpretation, but E and B were such a perfect pair for her work in every way, it seemed to me.

Then again I can see Bettina in the Kurt Jooss dance group or even with the José Limon dancers. Her sense of fluidity, line and nuances were imaged by Bettina into musical dance – effortless. ...

Notes

1. Beginning of my dance studies with Gertrud Bodenwieser, 1942 – Sydney.
2. Excerpts from a Bodenwieser dance program, 1940 – Sydney.
3. Dory Stern, pianist, accompanist, associate artist with Gertrud Bodenwieser in Australia, for her school and company 1941–1956 approximately. Excerpt from *Innovisions* by Coralie Hinkley. *Expressions of Creativity in Dance*. Cygnet books, published by the University of Western Australia Press. 1990.
4. *Vision*, choreography Gertrud Bodenwieser 1947; dancers: Elizabeth Russell, Coralie Hinkley.
5. *The New Dance* by Gertrud Bodenwieser, edited by Marie Cuckson. Private edition. Rondo Studios, Vaucluse, NSW Australia, p. 90.
6. 1942–1950; (1950–1953 performances in England with Mardi Watchorn and Elizabeth Russell); 1955–1957 rejoined Bodenwieser Dance Group in Sydney.
7. First Australian dancer to be awarded a Fulbright Scholarship for graduate study in USA with Martha Graham, Merce Cunningham, Doris Humphrey and Louis Horst. 1958, 1959 and 1960.
8. Doris Humphrey died in 1958; Gertrud Bodenwieser died in 1959.

17

BODENWIESER'S LAST FIVE YEARS

Marie Cuckson

Marie Cuckson writes of Gertrud Bodenwieser's continuing creativeness
up to the time of her death.

I first met Gertrud Bodenwieser in St. Mary's, a provincial "bush" town
in New South Wales, when my husband, Eric Cuckson, made her
acquaintance, almost by chance. She became keenly interested in the
social-industrial experiment which he was pursuing in his St. Mary's factory, the idea of which was to treat the whole personnel as a human community, not just a work force. My husband, who had known her work
in Vienna, persuaded Bodenwieser to interest herself in St. Mary's, and
she consented to give regular classes in the factory works theater. Our
announcement of the opening of the new school brought enough students for two classes straight away, and the young teenage group
became Bodenwieser's special interest.

Perhaps she met with a special response in that semi-rural, semi-
industrial township, where there was so little for the imagination; parents and friends crowded the far end of the hall every week to watch her
teach. Later, I was to realize that I too was as hungry for the excitements
of creative art as any of the rest of them, and I began to recognise the
unconscious symbolism in her work.

Bodenwieser's "St. Mary's girls", as she called them, became an
absorbing interest to her. They had never received any kind of dance
training, and almost all of them had never seen a professional dance
company of any kind. Far from being a drawback, it was this that
enabled Bodenwieser to form them in her own style and spirit from the
start, as she had done at the beginning of her career in Vienna. Within
four years, while still only in their mid-teens, they had become dancers
with true and recognizable "Bodenwieser" style and in her unique spirit.
She began to make choreographies for them, and several times brought
her professional company out from Sydney to perform on their stage.

This was the phenomenon: that once again, and for the last time,
and at this late time in her life, she had been able to inspire young girls to
unfold their creativity and to be, as dancers, mature in their expressiveness.

Once again, as it had been years before in Vienna, the improvisation became the highlight of each lesson and the means by which her pupils could become, themselves, creative in the language and spirit of Bodenwieser. Thus, as the new dancers developed, she reaffirmed the truth and validity of her art.

After five years, in 1959, she suffered a severe stroke, and her work was finished. Yet she recovered sufficiently to lead a quiet life for a few months until, on 10 November, another catastrophe killed her.

It was during these last few months that she and I drew near together, although I had been involved throughout with her work at St. Mary's. When she had recovered sufficiently, I had her to stay in our home, where we hoped she could be cared for and nursed gradually back to health. I felt anxious to preserve something of her heritage for the future, or at least to rescue it from the oblivion I seemed to foresee. She, with her instinct, felt the urge to use me for the same purpose, although neither of us said anything to that effect.

On one of these quiet last days, she asked me to help her to correct and complete her book. She had written in English, and there were a few awkward phrases, ambiguities, small omissions. I worked with her on the book and she completed it just before she died. She left in my hands the few photographs and papers she had saved in her flight from Vienna, and with these as a lead, I began my long task.

First, it was necessary to secure the future of the school at St. Mary's. Emmy Towsey (the former Emmy Steininger), who had danced for many years in the Bodenwieser Group, first in Vienna and afterwards in the Australian company, agreed to come out from Sydney to continue the training of Bodenwieser's special group of new dancers, until the growing school could be established with its own teacher–choreographer. The school is still continuing now in 1976, fifteen years later. It was Emmy Towsey more than anyone else who, gradually, over a long period, made it possible for me to learn and understand the past of Gertrud Bodenwieser and the significance of her place in dance. Whatever I learnt from others was measured and tested by reference to her, and she has worked with me to assemble and arrange the material that has been collected.

[From material held in the Hilverding Foundation.]

18

BODENWIESER'S FINAL MESSAGE TO YOUNG DANCERS

44   Gertrud Bodenwieser.

Young dancers of the present and of the future,
my last word is to you. Your way will be stony,
your path will be hard, but to you will one day
be the glory

> to have followed your convictions
> undeterred by material hardships
> or by the encasing wall of prejudice;

> to have fought in the great revolution
> of freeing the human mind;

> to have lifted up a great art and placed it
> on the pedestal of ethics,
> where it should stand,

> to have shown that we dance
> as we should endeavour to live:

IN TRUTH, SIMPLICITY AND SPIRITUALITY.*

The New Dance by Gertrud Bodenwieser, edited by Marie Cuckson. Private edition. Rondo
Studios, Vaucluse, NSW Australia, p. 98.

Reprinted from "The Sydney Morning Herald"
12th November, 1959.

Our Debt to
GERTRUD BODENWIESER'S ART
By A STAFF CORRESPONDENT

The final chapter in the life of Gertrud Bodenwieser, who died in Sydney on Tuesday, will form an inseparable part in the history of the art of the dance in Australia.

When she arrived in Sydney at the head of her Viennese group about 20 years ago, her fame as pioneer and prominent exponent of the "modern expressive" ballet was firmly established on a wide international plane.

In her native Vienna, she had built up a school around her name within the official Academy of Music and Dramatic Art which attracted students from all the corners of the world. The great theatrical producer Max Reinhardt was among the first to recognise the strength of her artistic innovations and frequently sought her cooperation as performer, choreographer and instructor. An ensemble of dancers, recruited from her students, carried her name all over Europe, then also to the Americas and the Far East.

Like Martha Graham, she based the choreography of all her dances on normal human posture and translated dramatic subjects, emotions and thoughts into movement without a stylised code. The dancers' bodies, from their hair down to their bare feet, had to be their sensitive, fully controlled instruments, be it in highly symbolistic tales or in simple unassuming pieces of entertainment.

An Influx
of Local Talent

When the political turmoil of the Hitler years made her decide to make Sydney her new home—she herself could have hardly expected how completely her work was to identify her with our own cultural scene.

The opening of her studio here placed so much talent into her hands that the Bodenwieser Ballet soon had to drop its acknowledgment to its Viennese origin. The school replenished throughout the years the ranks of her ensemble, particularly whenever one of her local graduates proceeded to further successes in England or the United States.

The Sydney-based Bodenwieser group achieved results unequalled by any similar body previously. They were the first major unit toured by the Arts Council all over this State—a venture so successful that it had to be repeated several times.

Soon there was no State within the Commonwealth where the "Bodenwiesers" had not been admired and applauded. Two tours to New Zealand marked their first conquests outside Australia. Soon they were followed by a tour to South Africa and another one to India. When the strain of such major undertakings proved too arduous for her, Bodenwieser adapted her methods to the medium of television, in which several of her presentations were featured.

Nothing but fanatical devotion to a cause could have kept Gertrud Bodenwieser's energies alive for so long—she was still demonstrating and dancing when she suffered her first heart attack last year. Despite her failing physical strength her mind was still obsessed with new ideas for new themes which, in the final phase, were reduced to nothing more than comforting dreams.

What will survive in most assertive form is the spirit of dedication which she has securely implanted in her many disciples, in Australia and in many other lands.

45 "Our Debt to Gertrud Bodenwieser's Art". *The Sydney Morning Herald* 12 November 1959.

CHRONOLOGY

Patricia Grayburn

1890	Gertrud Bondi born in Vienna on 3 February.
1905–1910	Traditionally assumed to have been taught to dance by Carl Godlewski, the first ballet master of the Vienna State Opera.
1910(?)	Assumed surname of Bodenwieser.
1919	First solo recital on 5 May.
1920	Became Course teacher in mime and dance at the Vienna State Academy of Music and Dramatic Art; married Friedrich Rosenthal, régisseur of the Burgtheater.
1922	First creation with a partner: *The Sister and The Man*.
1923	Formation of the Tanzgruppe Bodenwieser. Lengthy tours made annually until 1938 to many countries, including England (where she also lectured), and once to America.
1924/25	Karlheinz Martin commissioned Bodenwieser to choreograph two dramatic productions, Wedekind's *Franziska* and Klabund's *The Chalk Circle*.
1926	Programs of her work presented at the Austrian Embassy in London before the Duke and Duchess of York (the future King George VI and Queen Elizabeth); choreography for Goethe's *Faust* at the Burgtheater also taken to Berlin. Her dancers lent to Kurt Jooss for an oratorio. Kokoschka's *The Burning Thornbush* transformed into dance-drama, with music by Alex Tcherepnin. A second company created to cope with the many requests from impresarios.
1927	Max Reinhardt engaged Bodenwieser for *The Miracle* in the Circus Renz. She danced solo and also appeared with the group.
1928	The group appeared in *Der Schwarze Domino* by Auber and Bodenwieser choreographed dances for *Der Zarewitsch* by Lehár.
1929	Appearances at the London Coliseum in June and the Manchester Hippodrome in July.
1931	The group won first prize in the Riunione Internazionale di Danze in Florence.

1932	Took part with her group in the Concours de Chorégraphie in Paris and won a bronze medal. (The gold medal went to Kurt Jooss for *The Green Table*.)
1933	Gave course of lessons at the Rutherston Dubsky School in London.
1934	Group invited to Japan.
1936	*Sunset*. Last public appearance of Bodenwieser in Vienna.
1938	Annexation of Austria (*Anschluss*). Bodenwieser resigned her teaching position at the Academy and went to France, later joining her dancers in South America. They toured Colombia as *Revista Vienesa* for 10 months; Bodenwieser asked to stay on to teach and lecture.
1939	Outbreak of war; Bodenwieser (with Marcel Lorber) joined Shona Dunlop in Wellington, New Zealand, in May; in August reunited in Australia with six members of the Tanzgruppe (including Bettina Vernon and Evelyn Ippen) who were appearing in the revue *Around the Clock* in Sydney. In November the Company, now known as Bodenwieser Viennese Ballet, began touring Australia (and Tasmania), in due course under the auspices of C.E.M.A. (Council for the Encouragement of Music and the Arts, later the Arts Council).
1940	Friedrich Rosenthal seized by the Germans while trying to escape into Spain and sent to an extermination camp (died 1942?).
1940–1944	Bodenwieser Ballet contributed to the war effort by performing in aid of many causes, including shared programs with Colonel de Basil's Ballets Russes and Chico Marx of the Marx Brothers. Town Hall lunch-hour concerts in the big cities and open-air performances were among Bodenwieser's innovations. The members of the company, as well as Bodenwieser herself, began to teach in order to earn money.
1943	For the first time an Australian dancer (Innes Murdoch) danced the lead in a Bodenwieser Ballet (*The Pilgrimage of Truth*).
1944	Bettina Vernon and Evelyn Ippen, who had started a school in Rose Bay, Sydney, broke away from the Bodenwieser Group and formed their own group which was known either as *Viennese Dancers* or *Ballet for Two*, performing Bodenwieser dances and their own choreographies in the Bodenwieser style. Their places taken by Bodenwieser's Australian students.
1947	First tour of New Zealand by the Bodenwieser Ballet; Shona Dunlop, a New Zealander, having married Donald MacTavish, left to accompany him to China.

1947/48 *Ballet for Two* toured Japan giving performances for the Occupation Forces and charities. *Ballet For Two* brought the Bodenwieser style and dances back to Vienna at the Erstes Fest des Tanzes (First Festival of Dance) 1948 and toured the UK and Europe for many years.

1948 Bodenwieser Studio at 210 Pitt Street, Sydney, caught fire.

1949 Second tour of New Zealand with all-Australian cast.

1950 Four-month tour of South Africa.

1951 Male dancers included in the ballets for the first time.

1952 Tour of India.

1954 The St. Mary's Bodenwieser School set up at factory owned by Eric and Marie Cuckson, who cared for Bodenwieser after her first heart attack. Marie Cuckson and Emmy Taussig (Towsey) started Bodenwieser Archives.

1959 Death of Gertud Bodenwieser on 10 November after second heart attack. Buried in Darlinghurst. Memorial Recital performed by past and present dancers and students.

1970 Bodenwieser's manuscript *The New Dance* edited and published by Marie Cuckson, who also wrote a foreword. Margaret Chapple took over the direction of the Bodenwieser Dance Center in Sydney.

1979/80 "Dance in Vienna in the Twentieth Century" – an exhibition mounted by the Austrian Theater Museum, based on material from the Theater Collection of the Austrian National Library and from the Hilverding Foundation (donated to the Theater Collection in 1979).

   "Gertrud Bodenwieser" exhibition at Sydney Opera House.

1982 "Viennese Dance 1900–1960" – an exhibition initiated by Bettina Vernon mounted by the Austrian Institute and the Austrian Theater Museum at the Royal Festival Hall, London.

1988/89 Bodenwieser dances reconstructed by Bettina Vernon and Evelyn Ippen with MA students at the University of Surrey.

1989/90 Dr. Gerhard Brunner, Director of the Viennese State Opera Ballet and Artistic Director of the International Dance Festival, Tanz '90, invited Bettina Vernon and Evelyn Ippen to reconstruct Bodenwieser dances with dancers of the Vienna State Opera Ballet for performances at Tanz '90 and the Vienna State Opera House.

1990 Bodenwieser Centenary exhibition at University of Surrey, Guildford, and Royal Festival Hall, London. Initiated by Bettina Vernon and mounted by the Austrian Institute, London, and the Vienna Theater Museum. Sponsored by Bunzl plc.

Lecture by Dr. Gunhild Oberzaucher-Schüller: *Renaissance of the Viennese Modern Dance* at Sadler's Wells Theatre and University of Surrey.

1991   Illustrated lectures on Bodenwieser and Wiesenthal by Bettina Vernon and Evelyn Ippen at the Anglo Austrian Society and Manchester Festival. Live Study Demonstration directed by Bettina Vernon and Evelyn Ippen at Sadler's Wells Theatre, London.

1991/95 Illustrated lectures on Bodenwieser and Wiesenthal by Bettina Vernon at Birmingham, De Montfort, Leeds, Middlesex, Surrey, Salzburg and Vienna Universities and also at the English National Ballet School, the Royal Academy of Dancing and the Royal Ballet School.

1991   Class of the Bodenwieser style for students of the Royal Ballet School (White Lodge) by Bettina Vernon and Evelyn Ippen.

1993   Study Day on the Viennese School of Free Expressive Dance at the Institut Français, London, with the participation of Maria-luise Jaska, principal dancer, Vienna State Opera and Ballet, presented by the Austrian Institute London and the Society of Dance Research, arranged by Dr. Andrée Grau and Bettina Vernon.

1994/95 Reconstruction of "Terror" from the trilogy *The Masks of Lucifer* and Bodenwieser movements taught to students of the Bruckner Konservatorium, Linz, by Bettina Vernon and Evelyn Ippen for inclusion in Esther Linley's performance of *Tänze Der Verfemten* at Linz – and at the International Dance Festival in Vienna, 1996.

1995   Bettina Vernon died on 5 June, having suffered from cancer for more than thirteen years.
        Bettina Vernon-Warren Memorial Concerts given by Leslie Moorhouse (piano) at the Teikyo School, Fulmer, and Leighton House, London (in the presence of H.E. the Austrian Ambassador).

CHOREOCHRONICLE

Jarmila Weissenböck

Year	Title	Music
1919	*Silhouette (Scherenschnitt)*	F.C. Rheinhold
	Hysterie	M. Reger
	Spanischer Tanz	N. Rubinstein
	Cakewalk	C. Debussy
	Burletta	F.C. Reinhold
	Groteske	S. Rachmaninov
1920	*Ägyptische Impression*	C. Scott
	Faunischer Scherz	E. Poldini
	Pas de caractère	A. Glazunov
1921	*Prinzessin auf der Erbse*	E.W. Korngold
	Chinesischer Gaukler	L.M. Mayer
	Staccato und Legato	M. Reger
1922	*The Snow is dancing*	C. Debussy
	Aus dem Karneval	R. Schumann
	Sarabande	G.F. Handel
	Ein Wesen	C. Debussy
	Die Schwestern und der Mann	R. Schumann
1923	*Kubistischer Tanz*	E.A. MacDowell
	Ritterliches Kampfspiel	K.F. Horn
	Wichtelmännchen	E.W. Korngold
	Biblische Themen:	
	Frommer Auftakt	G.F. Handel
	Klageruf	E.A. MacDowell
	Das Hohelied	F. Petyrek
	Froher Ausklang:	
	"Es jauchzt die Erde..."	R. Strauss
	Freude	A. Schutt
	Die Nacht	A. Glazunov
	Frühling	Music Unknown
	Caprice	P.I. Tchaikovsky
	Festlicher Zug	R. Strauss

	"Der Verschwender"	
	by Ferdinand Raimund	K. Kreutzer
1924	*Gewalten des Lebens*	
	a. *Ein Wesen* (see 1922)	C. Debussy
	b. *Dämon Maschine / Demon Machine*	L.M. Mayer
	c. *Tanz um das goldenen Kalb*	F. Petyrek
	d. *Erlösung durch Güte*	M. Mussorgsky
	Die tragische und die heitere Maske	M. Mussorgsky, Lenne
	Gruppengroteske	F. Petyrek
	"Franziska" by Frank Wedekind	
1925	*"Der Kreidekreis" by Klabund*	K. Hiess
	"Aschenbrödel", pantomime – dances	
	"Paganini", operetta – dances	F. Lehár
1926	*Einleitender Chor*	
	"Berauschet euch ..."	Music Unknown
	Der brennende Dornbusch	A. Tcherepnin
	Tanzsuite:	
	a. *Lied*	
	b. *Burletta* (see 1919)	
	c. *Zwei Karikaturen*:	
	Girls	
	Exotisches (Exzentrisches)	
	Orchester	I. Stravinsky
	"Faust" by J.W. von Goethe	Music Unknown
	"Julius Cäsar", opera – dances	G.F. Handel
	Tänze nach russischer Musik:	Music Unknown
	Strassenlied	
	Intermezzo	
	Tartarenlieder	
1927	*Tänze nach alter Musik*:	
	Pavane	C.W. Gluck
	Gavotte	J.Ph. Rameau
	Prelude	A. Corelli
	Tänze nach neuer Musik:	
	Chansonette	Kaptylov
	Cakewalk (see 1919)	C. Debussy
	Ornamentale Bewegungsstudie	Music Unknown
	Spanischer Tanz	I. Albeniz
	Marsch	S. Prokofiev
	Volkslieder und Typen:	Music Unknown
	Rumänische Volksweise	
	Deutsches Weihnachtslied	

Arabische Strassentype
Tänze nach Wiener Musik:
  Ecossaise — F. Schubert
  Walzer — C.M. Ziehrer
  Polka — J. Strauss, the elder
  Galopp — J. Strauss, the elder
Tänze nach neuer Musik:
  Walzer — M. Reger
  Burletta — M. Reger
  Magie — S. Prokofiev
  Polka — A. Glazunov
  Marsch — S. Prokofiev
Passionsblumen/Waterlilies — E.A. MacDowell
Morgensblätterwalzer — J. Strauss
Pizzikato-Polka — J. Strauss
Clap hands! (*Charleston*) — J. Meyer
Marsch — F. Schubert
Menuett — W.A. Mozart
Serenade — J. Haydn
Marsch (*Der Schornsteinfeger*) — J. Strauss
Weihnachtslied (*Stille Nacht …*) — Traditional
Slawischer Tanz (*Ukrainisches Volkslied*) — J. Slavenski
Hokus-Pokus — K.D. von Dittersdorf
Tango — N. Gabe
Kujawiak — A. Wieniawski
Die fromme Helene tanzt black bottom — Music Unknown
Das alte und das neue Jahr — P. Linke
Künstlerleben — J. Strauss
Wiener Walzer — F. Schubert

1928   *L'Arlésienne* — G. Bizet
Konstruktivistisches Liebeslied — F. Poulenc
Strömung und Gegenströmung: — Music Unknown
  a. *Mystik*
  b. *Mechanisierung* (*Ford-System*)
  c. *Dekadenz*
"*Der schwarze Domino*" opera – dances — D.F.E. Auber
"*Der Zarewitsch*" operetta –
  Tscherkessentanz — F. Lehár
Exoten:
  a. *Chinesischer Gaukler* (see 1921) — L.M. Mayer
  b. *India* — V.I. Rebikov
Volkslieder: — Music Unknown
  Alt-Englisch

Schwedisch		
Slowakisch		
Steppenlied		
Gotische Suite:	C.W. Gluck	
Tanz der Schuld		
Tanz der Bitte		
Tanz der Gnade		
Seliges Schreiten		
Das himmlische Tor		
Relief	Music Unknown	
Rhythmen des Unbewussten:	E. Wellesz	
Präludium: Stille		
Traum vom Fliegen		
Traum der Lust		
Traum der Angst		
Epilog: Aufsteig zur Klarheit	M. Lorber	
Claire de lune	C. Debussy	
Heroischer Marsch	F. Schubert	
Der Rattenfänger von Hameln	F. Schubert	
Sinkende Dämmerung	E. Wellesz	
Steigendes Licht	M. Lorber	
Der säumige Freier oder		
Die Qual der Wahl /		
The Inconstant Prince	W.A. Mozart	
Eckiges Linienspiel (Gekreuzte Linien)	F. Poulenc	
Heraldischer Marsch	S. Prokofiev	
Valses nobles	F. Schubert	
Altorientalische Tanzparodie	Music Unknown	
Charlestonparodie	Music Unknown	
Tamburintanz	A. Glazunov	
Abendlied	E. Humperdinck	
Pierrette	C. Chaminade	
Aprilschauer	W. Weismann	
1929	*Amerikanischer Tanz*	I. Raudnitz
	Alla Turca	W.A. Mozart
	Tschinellentanz	M. Lorber
	Liebesfreud	F. Kreisler
	Wein, Weib und Gesang	J. Strauss
	Matrosentanz	J.P. Sousa
	Akrobatischer Scherz	E. Poldini
	Glocken/Swinging Bells	S.E. Bortkievicz
	Tangoparodie	M. Lorber
1930	*Die Geschichte vom armen Fischer*	S.E. Bortkievicz

	Fahnentanz/Flag Dance	R. Strauss
	Wer will Frau Wahrheit herbergen?	
	nach Hans Sachs/The Pilgrimage of	
	Truth (Ballet after the medieval guild-	S.E. Bortkievicz,
	play *Schwingungsaustausch*):	M. Lorber
	a. *Glocken* (see 1929)	
	b. *Sender und Empfänger*	
	c. *Ekstatische Kurve*	
	Delirienwalzer	J. Strauss
	Galopp	A. Casella
	Berceuse	A. Casella
	Drehtanz (Im Kreise)	F. Chopin
1931	*Das mittelalterliche Wien feiert*	
	die Vollendung und Eröffnung	
	seines Rathauses 1445	Music Unknown
	Olympische Spiele	R. Strauss
	Die grossen Stunden:	A. Tcherepnin
	a. *Schöpferische Stunde*	
	b. *Stunde der Erwartung*	
	c. *Stunde der Erfüllung*	
	Die Kugel	Music Unknown
	Jagdtanz der Diana	W.A. Mozart
	Gavotte	C.W. Gluck
	Warum	F. Schubert
	Glücks genug	F. Schubert
	Aufschwung	F. Schubert
	Im Fluge	F. Chopin
	Exzentriktänze:	
	Seltsame Gestalt	Music Unknown
	Modernes Spielzeug	Music Unknown
	Tanzweisen	W. Kienzel
	Chinesische Tänzer	W. Niemann
	Rosenkavalierwalzer /	
	Rosenkavalier-Waltzes	R. Strauss
	Till Eulenspiegel	R. Strauss
	Fast zu keck	M. Reger
	Clownerie	Music Unknown
	Cymbal Dance	J. Hawkins
1932	*Jazzbandparodie*	
	(see 1926: *Exotisches Orchester*)	I. Stravinsky
1933	*Rumba-Ekstase*	M. Lorber
	Asiatischer Tanz	M. Lorber

	Bunter Kranz	W. Kienzl
	Trigonometrie (Dreieck)	O. Schulhof
	Drei Tanzsymbole:	
	Das Nein	S.E. Bortkievicz
	Das Vielleicht	S.E. Bortkievicz
	Das Ja	M. Lorber
	Masken einer Fràu	M. Lorber
1934	*Wiegenlied der Mutter Erde /*	
	Cradlesong of Mother Earth	M. Lorber
	Beute/Booty (Sudanesischer Tanz)	J. Takacs
	Japanischer Schwerttanz	Music Unknown
	Der Karren / The Cart	M. Mussorgsky
	Der Abschied / The Farewell	M. Mussorgsky
	Tänze mit Tanzgeräten:	
	Tanz mit goldenen Scheiben /	
	Dance with golden discs	M. Lorber
	Tanz mit goldenen Reifen /	
	Dance with golden hoops	Music Unknown
	Dance of the Arabian Boys	A. Glazunov
	Bacchantischer Tanz	F. Chopin,
		F. Liszt
	Drehtanz	F. Chopin
	Sonnenuntergang / Sunset	K. Weigl
1935	*Das Ich*	A. Tcherepnin
	Das Du	A. Tcherepnin
	Im Garten des Rokoko	F. Gunther
	Romanze	P.I. Tchaikovsky
	Tanz der Hexe	M. Mussorgsky
	Damenturnriege 1900	Music Unknown
	"Wien bleibt Wien",	F. Salmhofer,
	spectacle – dances	C.M. Ziehrer
1936	*Die Masken Luzifers, Tanzdrama /*	
	The Masks of Lucifer,	
	Dance Drama	M. Lorber
	Stärke der Schwäche /	M. Labroca,
	Test of Strength	W. Baer
	Fahnentanz	C.W. Gluck
1937	*Österreichische Bauerntänze /*	
	Austrian Peasant Dances:	Traditional
	Schuhplattler	
	Polsterltanz	
	Ländler	
	Watschentanz	
	Neubäurische Polka	

1938	*Handwerkertanz*	M. Lorber
	Mariens Vision (Weihnachtslied /	
	Christmas Song)	Music Unknown
	The Mermaid (Die Nixe)	F. Chopin

Here ends Gertrud Bodenwieser's European Period.

1939	*Slavonic Dance*	A. Dvořák
	The Snakecharmer	C. Scott
1940	*Blue Danube*	J. Strauss
	The Sphinx	M. Lorber
	Gipsy Dance	M. Lorber
	Cinderella of old Vienna	J. Strauss
	Cain and Abel, Dance Drama	M. Lorber
	Greek Trilogy – Solos for the same Dancer	M. Lorber
	a. *Cassandra*	
	b. *Narcissus*	
	c. *Artemis*	
	I and Thou (see 1935)	A. Tcherepnin
	Hungarian Folk Dance	Traditional
	Memories of Vienna	J. Strauss
	Eve	N. Rimsky-Korsakov
	Hymn to the Flag	V. Bellini
1941	*Gothic Dance of the Crusades:*	C.W. Gluck,
	a. *Dance of Farewell*	M. Lorber
	b. *Dance of Gallant Fight*	
	c. *Dance of Prayer*	
	d. *Dance of Happy Reunion*	
	This is my Country's Sacred Soil	Russian Folksong
	Maria's Annunciation	Bach/Gounod
1942	*Narcissus* (see 1940)	M. Lorber
	Salome	R. Strauss
	Zephir	F. Liszt
	Pictures at an Exhibition	M. Mussorgsky
	A Cart drawn by Man (see 1934)	
	The Witches' Dance (see 1935)	
	Abandoned to Rhythm	S. Rachmaninov
	Puck	F. Mendelssohn
	Czechoslovakian Song	K. Hasler
	Parody of old Classical Ballet,	
	Pas de Deux	P. Linke
	Gossip	F. Mendelssohn
	Minuet	L. van Beethoven
	Danced Poems by E. Lambert	Music Unknown
	Mexican Village Serenade	Music Unknown

1943	*Epilogo*	E. Granados
	Caprice Viennois (Melody from Vienna)	F. Kreisler
1944	*The Wheel of Life*	M. Lorber
1945	*O World, Dance Drama*	A. Tcherepnin
	Trilogy of Joan of Arc:	M. Lorber
	a. *The Shepherdess receiving*	
	her great Message	
	b. *The Heroine in her Glory*	
	c. *The Martyr and the Saint*	
	Ritual Fire-dance	M. de Falla
	The Flight of the Bumble-bee	N. Rimsky-Korsakov
	The Night	F. Wilkens
	Songs my Mother taught me	A. Dvořák
	Scherzo-Tarantella	A. Wieniawski
1947	*The One and the Many*	W. Baer
1949	*The Life of the Insects, dance drama*	
	(After Karel Čapek's play)	W. Baer
1950	*We are so poor – we are so rich*	Czechoslovakian
		folksong
	The Wedding Procession	E. Grieg
	The Imaginary Invalid	
	(After Molière's play)	M. Lorber
	Melody from Vienna (see 1943)	F. Kreisler
	Grecian suite (see 1928: *Gotische Suite*)	C.W. Gluck
	a. *Dance of Guilt*	
	b. *Dance of Remorse*	
	c. *Dance of Mercy*	
	d. *Dance of Bliss*	
	e. *The Gates to Heaven*	
	Indian love song	Traditional
		Indian music
	Parody of Classical Ballet 1900	
	Period (Pas de Trois) (see 1942)	
1952	*The French Can-Can*	Music Unknown
	Arlequin et Colombine.	
	A Classical Ballet Pas de Deux	Music Unknown
1953	*Dance at Dusk (Indian Dance)*	E. Satie
	In Autumn	E.A. McDowell
1954	*Waltzing Matilda*	W. Baer
	Errand into the Maze, Dance Drama	G.C. Menotti
1956	*Trilogy of Central Australian Suite*:	C. Gheysens
	a. *Solitude*	
	b. *Wild Chase*	

	c. *A Child has been Born*	
	Aztec Woman's Prayer of Fertility	Mussilo
	Aboriginal Spear-Dance	C. Gheysens
	Indian Temple-Dance: Dance to Krishna	E. Satie
1957	*Blue Mist*	R. Cuckson
	Serenade to a Mask	C. Debussy
	Tarantella	J. Takacs
	Blue Mountain Waltz	C. Gheysens
	Waltz of Masquerade	A.I. Khachaturian

This list is far from complete and includes only a few of the great number of choreographies for her students. It is based on material from books, periodicals, press-cuttings, playbills and photographs available in the Theater Museum, Vienna, also in the Hilverding Foundation and the Austrian National Library.

The title of each choreography is quoted in the language in which it was first produced. A translation is given when it was performed later under this title.

The date of first performance is restricted to the year and has no claim to accuracy because of the great loss of documentation material in the second World War.

BETTINA VERNON-WARREN: A EULOGY

Christian Lanzer

We all feel sorrowful and that is natural when someone as lovely as Bettina is no longer with us in body. Sorrow and tears also have their place but let us remember that this is not only a Funeral Service – it is a Thanksgiving for a life of indomitable spirit, a thanksgiving that an illness bravely borne for so long is no more, a celebration of the life of Bettina, the adored wife, the much loved sister, the generous and affectionate aunt, and recently much to her delight a great-aunt, and of Bettina the dancer who achieved so much in her life-time, whose whole life from the age of five was a dream and a vision to dance and dance, a young girl who stood in awe of her brilliant teacher at the Vienna Academy, Gertrud Bodenwieser, that exponent of the Austrian School of Modern Expressive Dance, Bodenwieser who encouraged her young pupil, and at the same time disciplined her early exuberant dance steps, and when after some years the two met again in Australia their jubilation of seeing each other knew no bounds. Bettina with her future dance partner, Evelyn, became Bodenwieser's Principal Dancers and during the war years performed many of her dances, until in 1945, much to Bodenwieser's sadness and regret, both left her company and set up *Ballet for Two*, touring Australia, later on Japan and eventually brought it back to Europe with extensive tours under the Arts Council in the United Kingdom, then across they went to the Continent and their journeys reached an exciting climax when *Ballet for Two* performed as part of the first Festival of Dance (Fest des Tanzes 1948) in Vienna's Konzerthaus, the very place where Bettina first learned her art.

Several of their dances they choreographed themselves and one such is *Bonds of Harmony* of which we shall hear the music, one of Brahms's intermezzos.

And when the time came to dance no more Bettina was determined to repay some of the debt she felt she owed to her dance mistress by keeping Bodenwieser's name and style alive in her native Austria where of course she was less known because of the passage of time, and to ensure her due place amongst the great figures of Modern Dance of the 20s and 30s.

With unremitting energy and utter commitment Bettina set about researching, which in turn over the years led to writing about her subject, to helping to mount exhibitions at the University of Surrey, the Royal Festival Hall and Sadler's Wells Theatre, leading the seminars and lecturing widely.

The final step in reestablishing Bodenwieser's techniques came when Bettina and Evelyn were asked to reconstruct dances in Vienna for the State Opera Ballet, and thus *Demon Machine, Caprice Viennois* and *The Mermaid*, amongst others, performed by Marialuise Jaska and other principals, were received with enthusiasm by the Viennese audience. In all these events Charles was a constant support and adviser. Bettina's most recent engagement was for further reconstructions for the Esther Linley Ballet in Linz, but sadly she could no longer attend the first night; however, when Linz telephoned her with the good news that the performance was a great success and earned great audience acclaim, it brought much happiness to Bettina.

Other projects were being planned, amongst them a lecture in Moscow, but it was not to be. In all these events both the Austrian Institute and the Anglo-Austrian Society were of tremendous help, and without them all these exciting events would not have taken place.

Bettina was not without self-criticism. In an article about Bodenwieser she wrote 'Of all the great things Bodenwieser taught me, the greatest was absolute single-mindedness in my art, which, it is true, has led at times to criticism of me being oblivious to all else around me.'

Thinking back to our childhood days I remember that she endured school, rather than enjoyed it, but lived for her next session at the Academy, and I remember also the occasion when there were too many dandelions in the garden and our task was to cut off their heads, and so we set to work, but before long, sister was pirouetting around these cursed weeds, no doubt practising a new step, lost in her own dream world, and quite happily leaving her brother to do the humdrum decapitation. I must admit at that youthful age the brother did not appreciate that one had to make allowances for talent and such passion.

We all have our personal quirks – one of Bettina's was an agreement with me that despite the evidence of our birth certificates I would be the elder sibling, were I ever to be asked. As she herself always looked so very young, I did not feel it would do my own reputation much harm!

For the past thirty years she and Charles enjoyed Holly Cottage and there many visitors from home and abroad found their hospitality and friendliness a real tonic.

Their retirement was well earned, and even if it was not an idle one – Bettina found time to be an active member of the South Buckinghamshire branch of "WellBeing", for example, – it certainly was eventful for them both, and to us it seemed to be getting ever busier with more and more interest shown in her work.

One of her greatest pleasures was to be in Vienna – a city for which she had a protective love that would brook no criticism, and if one did dare to find fault, it was almost a personal insult, and a reproving look would come over her.

And so, I expect , all of us have personal memories to cherish, and we rejoice that she achieved all she set out to do – in her private life – happiness in her professional life – accomplishing her dream and her vision.

And for all that, and much else, we give thanks to Almighty God in this Service.

This eulogy was given by Christian Lanzer at the thanksgiving service for the life of Bettina Vernon-Warren at the Church of St James, Fulmer, on Friday 16 June 1995.

NOTES ON CONTRIBUTORS

Clement Crisp is dance critic of *The Financial Times*. In collaboration with Mary Clarke he has written a dozen books on various aspects of ballet and modern dance.

Helen Elton, first British student to receive State Diploma for Dancing and Physical Training in Vienna. Engaged by Grace Cone, Principal of the Arts Educational School in London, to teach the Bodenwieser Method of Dancing. Opened the Brooke Elton School of Dancing in London. Produced two ballets for the Jean Valmy Revue in Paris in 1937. Conducted Rhythmic Physical Exercises at a recreational center in Washington DC in the 50s.

Patricia Grayburn, read Modern Languages at Oxford. Head of Press and Public Relations at Royal Festival Hall, duties included working with London Festival Ballet. Arts Administrator, University of Surrey, since 1983. Member of the South East Regional Arts Board 1992–1996. Chairman Guildford Book Festival and Joint Executive Director Guildford International Music Festival. Trustee, Royal Ballet Benevolent Fund and Yvonne Arnaud Theater, Guildford. Council member, Friends of the Royal Academy of Arts.

In 1990 edited celebratory monograph on the 100th anniversary of Gertrud Bodenwieser's birth and mounted special exhibition at the University of Surrey in association with the Theater Museum, Vienna, and the Austrian Institute, London. Also showed exhibitions of the work of Grete Wiesenthal and Otto Wagner.

Coralie Hinkley, dancer, teacher, choreographer, author, poet. Formerly Bodenwieser Dance Company Sydney. Dance Recitals, London, own choreography; Recipient Fulbright Grant, USA 1958, 59, 60 – modern dance and choreography. Visiting Lecturer in Dance, Smith College. Received BS in Education, New York University. 1961 onwards introduced American modern dance techniques to dancers, educators, Bodenwieser colleagues in Sydney. Choreographer of Works – Ballet Australia. 1963–84, comprehensive dance education foundation programs in secondary and tertiary education. 1984 onwards, presenter Dance and Creativity International Conferences – Dance and the Child; World Council for Gifted and Talented. Continuing to dance and choreograph.

Choreographies include *Unknown Land, Day of Darkness, Eloges, The Forest, The Death of a Wombat, Ritual for Dance, Play and Magic*. Author of *Creativity in Dance*, 1980; *Innovisions*, 1990. Poetry: *Ashes of Roses* and *Spindrift*, 1991; *Through a Window*, 1993; *The Sky is Moving*, 1994; *Poetrix*, 1995. In *In Transit*, 1997, she makes an intimate, original and imaginative connection between dance and poetic images. Fifth generation Australian.

Evelyn Ippen, Bodenwieser dancer, teacher, examiner. Completed training at the Vienna Academy of Arts (Staatsprüfung). Joined the Bodenwieser Ballet for many tours and became a principal dancer, teacher and examiner. Toured Europe, Russia, Japan, America and Australia. Remained with the Bodenwieser Ballet in Australia until leaving in 1944 to form, with Bettina Vernon, their own group in which their own choreographies and Bodenwieser's were performed.

Returned to Europe via Japan and to England, having entertained the Occupation Forces in Japan. Based in England, toured the UK and Europe, taking part in Erstes Fest des Tanzes, 1948, in Vienna. Taught at universities and colleges in England.

Together with Bettina Vernon, reconstructed Bodenwieser dances with dancers of the Vienna State Opera Ballet for performances at the Wiener Internationales Tanzfestival, Tanz '90, Vienna State Opera House. Also reconstructed Bodenwieser movements and the dance *Terror* at the Bruckner Konservatorium, Linz for performances of *Tänze der Verfemten* at Linz and Vienna Festival of Dance 1996.

George Jackson, resident of Washington, DC, USA, has also lived in New York, Chicago, London, Cogenhoe and in Vienna where he was born. An ice figure skater as a child, he studied at the University of Chicago and became a writer (mostly on dance) and microbiologist (which has taken him to many places around the world). He was on the editorial staff of the literary magazines *Chicago Review* and *Venture*, chief editor of the scientific journal *Experimental Parasitology*, and currently reviews dance for *The Washington Post* newspaper and specialist magazines.

Christian Lanzer, born in Vienna, 1924, moved to England 1938; m. 1958 Juliet Creasy, four daughters. Education: Gymnasium, Vienna; Chatham House Grammar School, Ramsgate. London University B.A. (Hons). Assistant Master Chatham House Grammar School, Ramsgate; Senior Modern Language Master and Housemaster, Felsted School, Essex; Headmaster Bethany School, Kent. Retired 1988.

June Layson, after early Laban-based training, later studied at the Laban Art of Movement Center and taught at several British teacher-training colleges. In 1971 she was appointed to the University of Leeds to develop the first MA degree dance courses in the UK. In 1981 she became Head of the Department of Dance Studies at the University of Surrey, the first European university to establish a full range of graduate, post-graduate, doctoral degrees and post-doctoral research work in Dance. Her fields of interest are in dance history methodology and the development of British early modern dance, about which she has published widely. On her retirement in 1992 Professor Layson was awarded the title Emeritus Professor in recognition of her contribution to the study of Dance.

Innes Murdoch, born in Sydney, Australia, of English and Scottish parentage. Educated in Frensham, Mittagong, New South Wales, and taken to Europe by her parents in 1936. She felt very much at home in the lands of her forefathers, but returned to Sydney in 1939 and resumed dance training with Gertrud Bodenwieser. Innes Murdoch joined the Bodenwieser Ballet in 1941 and left in 1947 to marry the author W. H. Williams. They have three children.

In 1969 she started a Fine Arts Course at Sydney University and at the end of 1972 (together with her daughter) left Australia for an eight-month overland trip to England, via the Far East, India, Central Asia, the Middle East and Europe. She settled and lives in London, being interested in and occupied with further study, research, property development and extensive travelling.

Alfred Oberzaucher, a historian of the dance and ballet dramaturge of the Vienna State Opera, was editor of the journal *Tanzblätter* (with Gunhild Oberzaucher-Schüller). He wrote articles for several international dance periodicals and for Pipers *Enzyklopädie des Musiktheaters* (Munich), the *International Dictionary of Ballet* (Detroit, London, Washington D.C.) and the *International Encyclopedia of Dance* (Oxford, New York). He has also written scripts for television and video productions and adjudicated at choreography competitions.

Gunhild Oberzaucher-Schüller studied History of Theater and History of Arts at the University of Vienna and wrote a thesis on Bronislava Nijinska. Edited (together with Alfred Oberzaucher) the journal *Tanzblätter*. Was area researcher (Soviet Union) for *Choreography by Balanchine*. Is currently teaching Dance History at the Universities of Vienna (Austria), Bayreuth (Germany) and at the Conservatoire in Vienna. Has published numerous articles mainly on *Ausdruckstanz*, Ballets Russes, Russian Soviet Theater Avant-garde and 19th century ballet. Is editor of the dance section of Pipers *Enzyklopädie des Musiktheaters* (Munich), edited a reprint of the dance journal *Schrifttanz* (which launched Labanotation), and *Ausdruckstanz*.

Bettina Vernon (formerly Lanzer), 1920–1995. Dancer, choreographer, teacher and lecturer. Student of Gertrud Bodenwieser and Grete Wiesenthal at the Staatsakademie für Musik und darstellende Kunst in Vienna. In 1938 obtained the Akademie Diplom with the highest distinction for Künstlerischer Tanz. Joined the Bodenwieser ballet for performances in Australia from 1939 to 1944. Formed a partnership with Evelyn Ippen. Taught in and toured Australia and Japan before returning to Europe. Based in London they toured the UK and Europe, and danced at the Erstes Fest des Tanzes in Vienna, 1948. Reconstructed dances with the Vienna State Opera Ballet for Performances at the Vienna State Opera House and Tanz '90. They also reconstructed dances and taught Esther Linley's Group for performances at Linz and Wiener Internationales Tanzfestival, Tanz '96. She taught and lectured at universities and colleges in the UK, Salzburg and Vienna. Arranged for exhibitions to be held at Sadler's Wells Theatre, Royal Festival Hall and universities. At the time of her death invitations to lecture had been received from Moscow and Poland.

Charles Warren, MBE, DFC, MiD, on completion of training at the RAF College, Cranwell, was granted a permanent commission as a General Duties pilot in 1939. Joined a Fighter Command squadron and saw subsequent service as a Flight Commander at an Operational Training Unit, Bomber Command; with Transport Command in the Pacific; and as VIP pilot at the British Commonwealth HQ (AIR), Iwakuni, Japan. Retired in 1957 as Wing Commander. Married Bettina Vernon in 1951 and enjoyed supporting her in her many interests, in particular *Ausdruckstanz*.

Jarmila Weissenböck, born Vienna 1940, studied Theater and Art History at the University of Vienna. From 1971 librarian at the Austrian National Library. Since 1977 has been in charge of the Theater Collection of the Austrian National Library (which in 1991 became the Austrian Theater Museum). Adviser for autographs/literary papers, memorabilia and prints which included supervision of preparatory work on literary papers, memorabilia and personal effects of Hermann Bahr and Anna Bahr-Mildenburg, and also the Austrian puppeteer, Richard Teschner. Assistance was given with the reconstruction of the latter's performances. 1981–1990, supervised the work of converting the Lobkowitz Palace for housing the Austrian Theater Museum. Exhibitions mounted in Austria, London, New York, Milan and Havana. The subjects chosen were: Viennese Dance in the 20th Century, Gertrud Bodenwieser, Rosalia Chladek, Fanny Elssler, Yannis Kokos, Marcel Luipart, Meta Mettig – Dance in Bronze, Aurel von Milloss, Rudolph Nureyev, Riki Raab, Richard Teschner, Grete Wiesenthal and Christl Zimmerl. Lectures also given embracing many of the above.

INDEX

Other titles in the Choreography and Dance Studies series

This book is part of a series. The publisher will accept continuation orders which may be cancelled at any time and which provide for automatic billing and shipping of each title in the series upon publication. Please write for details.